**NORAH LOPEZ HOLDEN**
Regine Engstrand

TRAVIS
Jacob Engstrand

**Theatre credits include:** *Epic Love and Pop Songs* (Pleasance Dome) and *Mr Puntilla and His Man Matti, Pains Of Youth, In Arabia We'd All Be Kings, The Bright And Bold Design, The Winter's Tale, The Basset Table, Anthony and Cleopatra, Electra* (RADA).

**Radio work includes:** *A Charles Paris Mystery - The Cinderella Killer* (BBC Radio 4).

Will studied at the Royal Welsh College of Music and Drama.

**Theatre credits include:** *Fallen Angels* (Salisbury Playhouse); *Blind Date* (Touring); *Romeo & Juliet* (Pilot Theatre); *The Scarlet Pimpernel* (Fool's Gold Theatre Company); and *As You Like It, The Hound of the Baskervilles* and *A Midsummer Nights Dream* (Midsommer actors).

**Film credit includes:** *Dark River* (2017).

**KEN NWOSU**
Osvald Alving

**Television credits include:** *This is England* (Channel4); *Coronation St, Between the Sheets, The Second Coming, Where the Heart Is...* (ITV); and *The Accused, Torchwood* (BBC).

As a writer, Will's first piece *Monopoleyes* will be showing at The Kings Arms in Salford and Hope Mill Theatre on Tue 29 Nov – Sat 10 Dec.

**Trained at Drama Centre London**

Theatre credits include: *The Alchemist* (Royal Shakespeare Company & Barbican); *As You Like It* (National Theatre); *The Venice Season: The Merchant of Venice, Othello, The Roaring Girl Season: The Roaring Girl, Arden of Faversham, The White Devil* (Royal Shakespeare Company); *Perfect Match* (Watford Palace); and *A Human Being Died That Night* (Hampstead Theatre).

**Television credit includes:** *Shakespeare Lives – The Works* (BBC).

# GHOSTS
# IN
# REHEARSAL

# CREATIVE TEAM

## HENRIK IBSEN
### AUTHOR

Henrik Ibsen (1828–1906), Norwegian poet and playwright, was one of the shapers of modern theatre, who tempered naturalism with an understanding of social responsibility and individual psychology. His earliest major plays, *Brand* (1866) and *Peer Gynt* (1867), were large-scale verse dramas, but with *Pillars of the Community* (1877) he began to explore contemporary issues. There followed *A Doll's House* (1879), *Ghosts* (1881) and *An Enemy of the People* (1882). A richer understanding of the complexity of human impulses marks such later works as *The Wild Duck* (1885), *Rosmersholm* (1886), *The Lady from the Sea* (1888), *Hedda Gabler* (1890) and *The Master Builder* (1892), while the imminence of mortality overshadows his last great plays, *John Gabriel Borkman* (1896) and *When We Dead Awaken* (1899).

## DAVID WATSON
### ADAPTOR

David Watson's plays include *Pieces of Vincent* (Arcola/Paines Plough), *Flight Path* (Bush/Out of Joint) and *Just a Bloke* (Royal Court Young Writers Festival). He has written extensively for community and prison companies, with work including *Knife Edge* (Big House), *Housed* (Old Vic Community Company) and *Any Which Way* (Only Connect.) His short plays include *The Politician's Handbook* (Royal Court) and *You cannot go forward from where you are now* (Oran Mor/Paines Plough.) For television, he wrote for three series of *L8R* (Actorshop/BBC), for which he won three Children's BAFTAs. He wrote the screenplay for *The Hope Rooms* (Rather Good Film/Bill Kenwright Productions.)

## POLLY FINDLAY
### DIRECTOR

Polly was the joint winner (with Derren Brown) of the 2012 Olivier Award for Best Entertainment for *Derren Brown: Svengali*. She won the JMK Award for Young Directors in 2007, and was awarded the 2006/7 Bulldog Princeps Bursary at the NT Studio.

**Theatre credits include:** *The Alchemist* (Royal Shakespeare Company & Barbican); *As You Like It*, *Treasure Island*, *Protest Song* and *Antigone* (National Theatre); *Frøken Julie* (Aarhus Theatre, Denmark); *The Merchant of Venice* and *Arden Of Faversham* (Royal Shakespeare Company); *Krapp's Last Tape* and *A Taste of Honey* (Sheffield Crucible); *Gefährten/ Warhorse* (National Theatre & Theater des Westens, Berlin); *The Country Wife* and *Good* (Royal Exchange); *The Swan* and *Nightwatchman* (National Theatre & Paintframe); *Derren Brown: Svengali* (Shaftesbury Theatre); *Twisted Tales* (Lyric Theatre); *Honest* (Royal & Derngate & Milnes Bar, Edinburgh); *Light Shining in Buckinghamshire* and *Thyestes* (Arcola Theatre); *Eigengrau* (Bush Theatre); and *Romeo and Juliet* (Battersea Arts Centre).

## JOHANNES SCHÜTZ
### DESIGNER

Internationally acclaimed set designer Johannes Schütz has worked with directors of distinction such as Harald Clemen, Dieter Dorn, Hans Lietzau and Ernst Wendt.

**Recent theatre design credits include:** *The Merchant of Venice* (Royal Shakespeare Company), *Big and Small* (Barbican); *On the Chimborazo* (Münich Kammerspiele); *Mama and the Whore* (Schauspielhaus Bochum); *Katherine of Heilbronn* and *Summer Folk* (Düsseldorfer Schauspielhaus); *Who's Afraid of Virginia Woolf?* and *In the Greifswald Street* (Deutsches Theater Berlin); *Schiff Der Träume*, *Hysteria* and *Macbeth* (Düsseldorfer Schauspielhaus). Johannes also worked on numerous productions for the Salzburg Festival and Odéon-Théâtre de l'Europe in Paris.

Directing credits include: *Ariadne auf Naxos*, *Tristan und Isolde* (Kassel); and *Ariodante* (Salzburg Landestheater).

His publications include: *Stages 2000-2007* and *Johannes Schütz: Models & Interviews 2002-2015.*

## FRANZ PETER DAVID
### LIGHTING DESIGNER

Franz Peter David began his career in several German theatres, and was Lighting Designer and Head of the Lighting Department for Berlin State Opera 1994-2005. He has worked with designers including Hans Schavernoch, Johannes Schütz and Erich Wonder, directors including Ruth Berghaus, Luc Bondy, Götz Friedrich, Harry Kupfer, Johannes Schaaf and Robert Wilson, and choreographers Patrice Bart, Maurice Béjart and Vladimir Malakhov. Last year he lit *Der Rosenkavalier* for Baden-Baden Easter Festival, and has worked for opera and theatre companies in cities including Amsterdam, Brussels, Frankfurt, Hamburg, Beijing, Glasgow, Paris, Oslo, Tokyo and Zurich. For the Royal Opera, he lit *Le nozze di Figaro* for Johannes Schaaf and has designed lighting for *The Importance of Being Earnest.*

## EMMA LAXTON
### SOUND DESIGNER

**Previous work with HOME includes:** *The Oresteia.*

**Recent theatre credits include:** *Breaking the Code* (Royal Exchange); *Made in Dagenham* (Queen's Theatre & New Wolsey Theatre); *Boys Will Be Boys* (Headlong & Bush Theatre); *Observe the Sons of Ulster Marching Towards the Somme* (Headlong); *Great Expectations* (West Yorkshire Playhouse); *Elizabeth* (Royal Opera House); *The Effect* (Sheffield Theatres); *Henry the Fifth* (Unicorn Theatre, Imaginate Festival); *All My Sons* (Talawa); *Accolade* (St James Theatre); *Pests* (Clean Break and Royal Court); *Coriolanus* (Donmar Warehouse); *nut* and *Men Should Weep* (National Theatre); *Black T-Shirt Collection* (Fuel UK Tour & National Theatre); *Much Ado About Nothing* (West End).

Emma designed twenty productions during her time as Deputy Head of Sound at the Royal Court Theatre.

## MARC TRITSCHLER
### COMPOSER/ARRANGER

Marc is a pianist, MD, music supervisor, arranger and composer of music for the theatre.

**Theatre credits include:** *A Pacifist's Guide to the War on Cancer* (Complicite); *As You Like It* (National Theatre); *The Merchant of Venice* (The Royal Shakespeare Company); *The Wyld, Show Me* (Friedrichstadt-Palast, Berlin); *Warhorse* (Theater des Westens, Berlin) and *We Will Rock You* (Germany, Switzerland, Sweden and Belgium).

He is also the founder and artistic director of the Berlin-based music label Testklang.

## PETRA JANE TAUSCHER
### DRAMATURG

Petra studied at Oxford University and at the Ernst Busch Academy of Dramatic Art in Berlin. She spent her first professional years in Europe: three years with Peter Stein, then at the Berlin Ensemble. Returning home to the UK, she had an opportunity to work in film and later became Head of Drama at Atlantic Productions. Petra is a member of the in-house producing team and dramaturg on all HOME produced shows.

## SAMUEL WARD
### ASSISTANT DIRECTOR
**(Birbeck MA in Theatre Directing)**

Sam is the Resident Assistant Director at HOME. He is currently studying for a masters in Theatre Directing at Birkbeck in London. Prior to that he directed 10 shows over three years in Oxford and at the Edinburgh Fringe, with a combination of devised work and contemporary plays from writers such as Philip Ridley, Sarah Kane and David Greig. His new company YESYESNONO opens its debut piece at Camden People's Theatre in January.

# PRODUCTION TEAM

## STAGE MANAGEMENT

**JAMIE BYRON**
Company Stage Manager

**PHILIP HUSSEY**
Deputy Stage Manager

**CLARE LOUISE HEATH**
Assistant Stage Manager

## TECHNICAL

**RICHARD OWEN**
Production Manager

**ANDY SMITH**
Head of Lighting, Sound and Video

**KEITH BROOM**
Technical Manager

**HELEN HALL**
Deputy Technical Manager

**PAUL GREGORY**
Sound Supervisor

**DANNY STEWART**
Lighting Supervisor

**MELISSA ASHLEY**
Lighting, Sound and Video Technician

**KEVIN WILLIAMS**
Lighting, Sound and Video Technician

**MARK McKENNA**
Stage & Event Technician

**DAVE DOYLE**
Stage Supervisor

**AVRIL MASON**
Production Administrator

**ALISON CARTLEDGE**
Costume Supervisor

**NIKKI WRAGG**
Wardrobe Assistant/Dresser

## FOR HOME

**JASPER GILBERT**
Technical Director and Head of Production

**KEVIN JAMIESON**
Senior Producer

**JODIE RATCLIFFE**
Assistant Producer: Theatre

## SPECIAL THANKS

HOME Volunteers for all their commitment to HOME, Bolton Octagon, The Dukes, Lancaster, Oldham Coliseum, Royal Exchange Theatre, Theatre Clwyd, Mold and Sheffield Theatres.

# OUR HOME IS YOUR HOME

## ACCESS

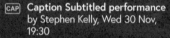 **Caption Subtitled performance** by Stephen Kelly, Wed 30 Nov, 19:30

**BSL Interpreted performance** by Alex McDonald, Thu 1 Dec, 19:30

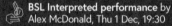 **Audio Described Touch Tour** by Mind's Eye, Sat 3 Dec, 13:00

**Audio Described performance** by Mind's Eye, Sat 3 Dec, 14:00

## POST SHOW DISCUSSION

**Thu 1 Dec**

Free to *Ghosts* ticket holders

Join us for a post-show discussion following the show on Thu 1 Dec with director Polly Findlay and members of the cast.

Presented in association with CIDRAL, University of Manchester.

## PLAYREADING

HOME's regular Playreading group meets on the first Friday of each month from 10:45 – 12:45. Anyone is welcome and no experience is necessary. Book tickets on the website or via Box Office.

## FAMILIES

Bring the family to your HOME from home. This regular programme includes exciting performances, wacky workshops and alternative films for all the family to enjoy on Sundays. Check our website for details of up and coming events. We recommended booking early to avoid disappointment. **homemcr.org/families**

## CREATIVES

Spotting, developing and showcasing the work of local artists and creatives is a big part of our work at HOME. We have plenty of skills development workshops and courses throughout the year, plus networking sessions and open submission opportunities to get your work shown. Check **homemcr. org/creatives** for information on what's coming up.

## SCHOOLS & COLLEGES

Our annual Schools & Colleges programme uses film, visual arts and theatre to enrich students' learning.

Events cover Modern Foreign Languages, Film & Media, Visual Arts, Drama and English and are mostly aimed at the 14-19 age group studying GCSE, AS, A2 and equivalent. We can also provide school groups with tours of the venue throughout the year on request. For full programme details, visit **homemcr.org/schools**

## HOME YOUNG CREATIVES

HOME Young Creatives is our programme run by and for 15-25 year olds who are into art, film and theatre. Every year, we'll be putting on an amazing series of free workshops, projects and commissioning opportunities which will be led by industry professionals. For further information, sign up to the HYC newsletter at **homemcr.org/HYC**

**For more information on any of these events, visit homemcr.org, or contact the Box Office on 0161 200 1500**

# NAME A SEAT AT HOME

As a registered charity, we depend on the generosity of our friends and loyal audiences. Each year we need to raise over £600,000 to ensure HOME is open to as many people as possible.

For a donation of £250 or more, you can commemorate a special occasion or remember a loved one by commissioning a plaque in our main theatre or any of our cinemas.

Plaques remain in place for a minimum of 10 years.

*Having a plaque on a seat is more than just seeing my name in public: it identifies my commitment to a place where I feel welcome and comfortable. I'm at "HOME".*

Wyllie Longmore

*Our dear friend Jonathan watched the building of HOME from his apartment... he would have visited the cinemas and the theatre (and the bar!) with us. It feels good to have a seat in his name plus one for his guest so we can remember him and his love of the Cornerhouse and Library Theatre.*

Denise Drury

To find out more about dedicating a seat please call Michelle Nicholson, Development Administrator on **0161 212 3429** or drop her an email at: **michelle.nicholson@homemcr.org** You can also visit us at **homemcr.org/individual-giving**

# HOME

# COMING SOON...

Little Angel Theatre presents

## WOW! SAID THE OWL

### WED 14 – FRI 30 DEC

This Christmas, explore the wow-world of colours with this curious little owl who is determined to stay awake to see what day light brings

Recommended for children aged 2 – 5.

Box of Tricks presents

## NARVIK

### TUE 31 JAN – SAT 4 FEB

A new play with songs by Lizzie Nunnery, *Narvik* tells the story of a Liverpudlian man and a Norwegian woman pulled together and torn apart by war as the events of one summer cause ripples across an ocean of time.

59 Productions, HOME and Lyric Hammersmith presents Paul Auster's

## CITY OF GLASS

### SAT 4 – SAT 18 MAR

Tony Award-winning 59 Productions (*War Horse*) and award-winning writer Duncan Macmillan (*1984*) bring this seminal American novel to life in a dazzlingly original stage adaptation.

FUNDED BY

MANCHESTER CITY COUNCIL · ARTS COUNCIL ENGLAND · AGMA · EUROPA CINEMAS

OFFICIAL TECHNOLOGY PARTNER
BUSINESS

OFFICIAL HOTEL PARTNER
INNSIDE MANCHESTER

FOUNDING SUPPORTERS

The Granada Foundation · Transport for Greater Manchester · University of Salford MANCHESTER · MANCHESTER SCHOOL OF ART

# Ghosts

Henrik Ibsen (1828–1906), Norwegian poet and playwright, was one of the shapers of modern theatre, who tempered naturalism with an understanding of social responsibility and individual psychology. His earliest major plays, *Brand* (1866) and *Peer Gynt* (1867), were large-scale verse dramas, but with *Pillars of the Community* (1877) he began to explore contemporary issues. There followed *A Doll's House* (1879), *Ghosts* (1881) and *An Enemy of the People* (1882). A richer understanding of the complexity of human impulses marks such later works as *The Wild Duck* (1885), *Rosmersholm* (1886), *The Lady from the Sea* (1888), *Hedda Gabler* (1890) and *The Master Builder* (1892), while the imminence of mortality overshadows his last great plays, *John Gabriel Borkman* (1896) and *When We Dead Awaken* (1899).

David Watson's plays include *Pieces of Vincent* (Arcola/Paines Plough), *Flight Path* (Bush/Out of Joint) and *Just a Bloke* (Royal Court Young Writers Festival). He has written extensively for community and prison companies, with work including *Knife Edge* (Big House), *Housed* (Old Vic Community Company) and *Any Which Way* (Only Connect.) His short plays include *The Politician's Handbook* (Royal Court) and *You Cannot Go Forward from Where You Are Now* (Oran Mor/Paines Plough.) For television, he wrote for three series of *L8R* (Actorshop/BBC), which he won three Children's BAFTAs. He wrote the screenplay for *The Hope Rooms* (Rather Good Film/Bill Kenwright Productions).

HENRIK IBSEN

# Ghosts

*or*

Those Who Return

*a version by*

DAVID WATSON

*from a literal translation by Charlotte Barslund*

FABER & FABER

First published in 2016
by Faber and Faber Limited
74–77 Great Russell Street
London WC1B 3DA

Typeset by Country Setting, Kingsdown, Kent CT14 8ES

Printed and bound by CPI Group (UK) Ltd, Croydon, CR0 4YY

A CIP record for this book
is available from the British Library

ISBN 978–0–571–33673–9

2 4 6 8 10 9 7 5 3

**Ghosts** in this version was first performed at HOME, Manchester, on 18 November 2016. The cast, in alphabetical order, was as follows:

**Pastor Manders** Jamie Ballard
**Helen Alving** Niamh Cusack
**Regine Engstrand** Norah Lopez Holden
**Osvald Alving** Ken Nwosu
**Jacob Engstrand** William Travis

*Designer* Johannes Schütz
*Lighting Designer* Franz David
*Sound Designer* Emma Laxton
*Composer/Arranger* Marc Tritschler
*Dramaturg* Petra Jane Tauscher
*Assistant Director* Samuel Ward

# Characters

**Helen Alving**
widow of Captain Alving

**Osvald Alving**
her son, an artist

**Pastor Manders**

**Jacob Engstrand**
a carpenter

**Regine Engstrand**
in Mrs Alving's service

*Setting*

Mrs Alving's estate, by a large fjord
in the middle of the countryside

# GHOSTS

# Act One

*A large garden room, in the middle of which is a circular table surrounded by chairs. On the table there are books, magazines and newspapers – it's a mess.*

*A sofa, and a work table. A television, which is switched on.*

*Upstage, the room extends into a somewhat smaller conservatory, with glass walls and large windows. A gloomy fjord landscape beyond, and the sounds of a lonely port close by, as well as of heavy rainfall.*

*Engstrand, a carpenter, is entering via the garden door. He limps a bit on his left leg.*

*Regine, holding an empty flower spray, enters – she stops when she seems him.*

**Regine** What do *you* want?!

**Engstrand** Oh – what a welcome, Regine, I'm underwhelmed.

**Regine** Don't make yourself at home in here, Osvald – (*Corrects herself.*) Mr Alving's asleep upstairs.

**Engstrand** You what?

**Regine** Shhh!

**Engstrand** It's two in the afternoon!

**Regine** So?

**Engstrand** O-four-hundred I got in last night, or should I say this morning, caning it I was, and two hours later? Up with the sun, mate. Up to work.

**Regine** Much as I'd like to parlay-vous –

**Engstrand** Oh, simmer yourself fucking down, I won't stop long.

**Regine** I don't want anyone seeing you here so please don't.

**Engstrand** Orphanage is finished – Thank you, Carpenter Engstrand.

**Regine** Orphanage?

**Engstrand** Alright, children's home. Now that means every Billy Big-Bollocks from here to town'll be making his way out here tomorrow night for the what's-it. Blessing.

**Regine** And?

**Engstrand** And, there will be on offer, a certain amount of what are known as cold beverages. Which means I am straight back into town tonight, no danger.

**Regine** You surprise me.

**Engstrand** Then let no one say that Jacob Engstrand's not able to hold his own, in the face of temptation.

**Regine** Well, bon voyage.

*A short pause.*

**Engstrand** Pastor Manders'll be down.

**Regine** He's down today, so what?

**Engstrand** Show meself up in front of him? No chance.

**Regine** Oh, so that's what this is.

**Engstrand** Eh?

**Regine** What are you scheming him into this time?

**Engstrand** 'Scheming him i—' Are you cracked? That man's been good to me.

**Regine** D'accord.

**Engstrand** 'Scheming him i—'

**Regine** Was there something you wanted to say?

**Engstrand** I've a mind to not say it now.

**Regine** See you then.

**Engstrand** Listen.
I'm back into town tonight –

**Regine** The sooner the better.

**Engstrand** – and so are you.
I want you home with me, Regine, time's come.

**Regine** You what?

**Engstrand** Now . . .

**Regine** Not in a trillion years am I coming back into town with you.

**Engstrand** Listen –

**Regine** After all this time under the Alvings' roof, and treated as one of their own?

**Engstrand** Oh yeah?

**Regine** What, throw all that away, should I, and back to the likes of you?

**Engstrand** Oh, setting up against your old man now is it?

**Regine** You said often enough I'm no problem of yours.

**Engstrand** That was the drink talking!

**Regine** Cold-hearted bitch, I think it said.

**Engstrand** Oh . . . And your mother. Giving it the fucking violin routine. 'Oh get away from me, Jacob, I served under Captain Alving three years!' And didn't we know it!

**Regine** Well a nice early grave you made for Mother anyhow, so never mind.

**Engstrand** Oh, pin that on me is it?

**Regine** And that leg.

**Engstrand** What did you say?

**Regine** Pied de mouton.

**Engstrand** 'Pied de mouto—' What's that then, fucking . . . English?!

**Regine** Yeah.

**Engstrand** Well –
　　Good. That is good, you've had some education here, and that'll come in handy now –

**Regine** With you, in town? What d'you want me there for anyway?

**Engstrand** What kind of a father wouldn't want his only child?!

**Regine** You tell me.

**Engstrand** I'm . . . lonely, and . . . a widower, is what I am –

**Regine** Amongst other things.

**Engstrand** The truth is –
　　This job's been a touch for me, I'm flush at the minute, and let's face it, I mean there's fuck-all a' spend your money on out here –

**Regine** Will you watch your mouth?

**Engstrand** Yes. Yep. Bad habits – knock 'em dead, I make you right there –

**Regine** So you've money.

**Engstrand** Which I have been putting aside, with an eye towards . . . a new venture. In town.

**Regine** A venture.

**Engstrand** Fair play, I know, I have . . . ventured, before. But this is watertight.

**Regine** Is it?

**Engstrand** Got me eye on a spot, down the port sort of thing, empty warehouse, you know, buy it up, convert it.

**Regine** Oh yeah?

**Engstrand** Into a sort of a . . .
  Well, a bar.
  With some . . . entertainment . . .
  Bit of a dance . . .

**Regine** Whereabouts?

**Engstrand** I told you, in town.

**Regine** Whereabouts in town?

**Engstrand** Just . . . round the fucking / port –

**Regine** Oh, round the fucking port is it?

**Engstrand** It's Little Harbour Street.

**Regine** Oh, my God –

**Engstrand** Now you hear me out –

**Regine** I know what kind of bars there are in Little Harbour Street –

**Engstrand** Yeah, well, you don't know this one, right, I'm talking officer class –

**Regine** And how exactly do I fit into all this?

**Engstrand** Pretty well, mate, I should say, an easy life. These . . . sailors and . . . Honestly, they're a bit a' class, these, erm . . . seafaring types we'll be mostly catering for, and . . . and they like a woman's touch –

**Regine** I bet they do –

**Engstrand** Oh, look at yourself out here.
So she's taught you French and English, whoopy-do, but what now?
That kiddies' home. She'll bung you in there with those pikey little . . . before you can say bon-fucking-jour.

**Regine** Maybe.
Or maybe something else'll occur.

**Engstrand** Oooh . . . 'Something else'll occur,' she says –

**Regine** A lot of money you've saved is it?

**Engstrand** Eight hundred and fifty kronar.

**Regine** That's not bad.

**Engstrand** A start, 's what it is.

**Regine** And how much of it's mine?

**Engstrand** 'How much of it's mine'? Jog on.

**Regine** You wouldn't think of sending me some towards . . . a new top, or –

**Engstrand** You come with me to town you'll have tops!

**Regine** Oh, I'll buy me own.

**Engstrand** You wouldn't be with me for long.

**Regine** Wouldn't I?

**Engstrand** You're a good-looking girl these days, who's to say a young officer, a captain, might come along . . . slip summat down your ring-finger –

**Regine** Marrying sailors now, it gets better and better, this.

**Engstrand** Well don't marry 'em then!
   That Englishman.
   With the yacht.
   Six hundred kronar he paid, and she were no better looking than you –

**Regine** (*advancing on him*) Get out!

**Engstrand** Oh, raise your hand to me is it –

**Regine** Talk about Mother again I will raise my fucking hand. Now get out! Out!
   And don't slam the door, Mr Alving / is asleep upstairs

**Engstrand** Is asleep, yes, you're very concerned with the young Mr Alving, I'm half-inclined to think –
   Oh, shame. Is he the something else that might occur, is he?

**Regine** Get out of here!

**Engstrand** Oh, Regine.

**Regine** Not that way, Pastor Manders is coming!

**Engstrand** (*on his way out*) I'll have him have words with you, the Pastor. About the duty a daughter owes her old man. And I am your old man all the same, Regine, you get yourself down the town hall, you can check!

   *Pastor Manders enters.*

**Manders**  Miss Engstrand.

**Regine**  Oh, well look who's here. Good morning, Pastor! Is the boat in already?

**Manders**  It is. And it's still raining.

**Regine**  Keeps the farmers happy.

**Manders**  (*in agreement*) The farmers.
     (*Taking off his overcoat.*) Townies like me, we never see beyond ourselves.

**Regine**  Oh let me give you a hand. You're soaked!

*A little self-consciously she helps him off with his jacket.*

I'll hang it up in the hall and open out your brolly.

**Manders**  All's fine here?

**Regine**  Yes, thank you.

**Manders**  You must be busy, for tomorrow.

**Regine**  Yes, there's quite a lot still to do.

**Manders**  And Mrs A is home, I hope?

**Regine**  She is. She's erm – ironing shirts, for the young master.

**Manders**  The 'word on the street', is the young master arrived early.

**Regine**  Yes. Yes, he came the day before yesterday. He surprised us.

**Manders**  Is he well?

**Regine**  Yes, he is, thank you. Though very tired, from the journey, he came straight through.
     I mean he came direct.

In actual fact I think he's still asleep at the minute,
so . . . we might be best to talk just a teensy bit more
quietly.

**Manders**  Oh, we'll be very quiet.

**Regine**  Are you comfy enough, Pastor?

**Manders**  I am quite comfortable, Regine, thank you.
You've changed since I saw you last, I think.

**Regine**  Oh yes?

**Manders**  You've grown.

**Regine**  Mrs A says I'm looking well these days.

**Manders**  I would say you're looking very well.

*A pause.*

**Regine**  Perhaps I should tell Mrs Alving you're here?

**Manders**  No rush.
How is your father, Regine?

**Regine**  Thank you, Pastor, he's well.

**Manders**  He looked me up when he was last in town.

**Regine**  Oh yes?
Yes, he's always very pleased, to have had a chat with
you.

**Manders**  You see him often?

**Regine**  Erm. When I have the time, I . . .

**Manders**  He's no strong man, your father, Regine. He's
needed a, erm . . . a guiding hand, it seems to me, for
quite some time.

**Regine**  Yes.

**Manders** He needs someone around him he can relax with, whose opinion he can trust. He said as much the last time we spoke.

**Regine** He mentioned that to me too, Pastor Manders.

Though I doubt that Mrs Alving would be too keen on seeing the back of me, and . . . especially what with the children's home, to think of, and . . . and I'd be loath to leave Mrs Alving myself, she's always been very kind to me.

**Manders** Yes, that's true.

Yes, I understand the sentiment, but there is also a daughter's duty, Regine.

**Regine** Yes.

**Manders** I'm sure Mrs Alving would understand that.

*A slight pause.*

**Regine** I don't know that it would be the right thing for a girl of my age to keep house for a single man.

**Manders** We're talking about your father.

**Regine** Yes. Yes, I suppose we are.

But if it were a nice house, do you know what I mean? For a real gentleman.

Someone I could be devoted to and look up to, and . . . and almost take the place of a daughter for –

**Manders** (*half laughs*) Regine . . .

**Regine** Then I might feel more inclined, to go back into town.

**Manders** 'Inclined', she says. As if it's a choice, to be made . . .

**Regine** It can be quite lonely out here.

The Pastor must know how loneliness feels.

I think in that case I'd be more than eager . . .
Perhaps the Pastor might know, of a situation –?

**Manders** I don't know of a situation of that kind, Miss Engstrand, no.

*A slight pause.*

**Regine** Or perhaps, if he could keep me in mind . . .

**Manders** Perhaps you could fetch Mrs Alving now.

**Regine** Yes.
She'll be here right away, Pastor.

*Regine exits. A short pause. Helen Alving enters, followed by Regine, who immediately re-exits back into the house.*

**Helen** Here you are.

**Manders** Here I am. As promised.

**Helen** On absolute perfect time as always.

**Manders** Which was quite an achievement, believe you me, the amount of people and problems piling up on my plate these / days.

**Helen** Well, all the more nice of you to be punctual. We can get things over with before lunch.

**Manders** Yes.

**Helen** Where are your bags?

**Manders** At the grocer's house, I'll stay there tonight.

**Helen** And after all these years you still won't share a roof with me.

**Manders** It's convenient. To be down there with the boat close by.

**Helen** Oh Pastor, not even for just one night? We're oldies, the both of us now, we don't need to worry about . . . convenience and dreary things like that.

**Manders** I can tell you're in good spirits.

**Helen** Good spirits. That's not the half of it.

**Manders** And why not? A travelling son's come home. And tomorrow, a celebration.

**Helen** It's been two years. And do you know, he's promised to stay with me the whole winter.

**Manders** There you go. Take that, Berlin . . . Bangalore . . .
Charms you may well have, but you are no match for a sacred filial bond.

**Helen** Well, I'm not sure what that means but I know he has his mother here.
He's come home to me.

**Manders** The . . . arty-farty world is not so strong as to blunt his natural inclinations.

**Helen** The arty-farty world is not so strong as . . . No, I suppose it's not.
He'll be down soon, he's only having a nap.

**Manders** Is now a good time to –?

**Helen** Yes. Let's.

**Manders** Right then.

*He begins to assemble his papers.*

**Helen** I wonder if you'll recognise him, after all this time.

**Manders** (*surveying the mess*) I see you've finally got the place looking just how you like.

**Helen** We've been busy.

**Manders** I know.

**Helen** Are those the documents?

**Manders** These are them. I had to push, believe you me, to have them ready in time, the amount of red tape there is for a thing like this –

*She is looking intently at the documents.*

But the, er. Yes. The registered deeds to Solvik Farm. Dormitories, classrooms, staff quarters and chapel. All listed. All approved.
 And the articles of appropriation here, look, for the – Captain Alving Home for Children.

**Helen** So this is it.

**Manders** It is. And here's the savings book for the interest, it's set aside to cover the running costs, of the home.

**Helen** Right. Can you hang on to all this, for now?

**Manders** I can.
 Er – suggestion – we keep the money in savings, for the minute.
 Interest rate's not looking too clever, and . . . But we'll keep an eye out. Then down the line we'll get a mortgage together, a good one, you know.
 And we'll take it from there.

**Helen** I'll trust your opinion, Pastor.

**Manders** Thank you, Helen.

**Helen** Right.

**Manders** There is one more thing.

**Helen** What's that?

**Manders** I've been meaning to ask –
Do you want to have the place insured?

**Helen** Well of course I do, it has to be.

**Manders** Well.
Yes –

**Helen** Everything's insured, the house, the . . . out-buildings –

**Manders** It's –

**Helen** Everything on the estate.

**Manders** Exactly. On *your* estate. As is everything on my humble . . .
But you could say that the children's home is a part of a wider . . . context.

**Helen** I don't follow.

**Manders** Helen – if it were down to me . . .
I'd be quite happy, pragmatically, to . . . safeguard against all outcomes, but . . .
An institution. Designed for the work of God.
Now there are some who would look at that and think 'In that case – is it not God's protection alone . . . that should serve?'

**Helen** Yes, I see.

**Manders** And that is not my opinion, as I say, and it is not anyhow my decision to make, but there are those who would look upon a choice like that, and . . . it's a tricky one, Helen.
Because these people –

**Helen** Yes, I know the type.

**Manders** They wouldn't be slow to voice any kind of objection, to you . . . I mean even to me! . . .

And to think, that they'd think, that we . . . I don't know, that we hadn't sufficient . . . faith, as it were, in a higher authority.

**Helen** But you and I both know . . .

**Manders** Oh, our conscience is . . . cleaner than the best of them!
But can you imagine . . .
I mean it's not gone unnoticed, the home, by any means, the town is full of how it'll ease the council's burden in terms of . . . Because of course it'll take in those from all over –

**Helen** Yes, perhaps we'd better leave it then.

**Manders** Is that what you want?

**Helen** Is it?

*A slight pause.*

**Manders** If an accident were to happen. Could you cover it?

**Helen** No, I can tell you now that I couldn't do that.

**Manders** You realise, Helen, the responsibility –

**Helen** But then what's the alternative?

**Manders** Well this is it, I mean we're damned, as it were, if we do, and . . .
Faith, is what we need, in trusting the home to its rightful . . . overseer, and . . . and all the special protection the place, God willing . . . that such a place is granted.

**Helen** Right. God willing.

**Manders** Shall we leave it then?

**Helen** Let's.

**Manders** (*nods*) If that's what you want. (*Makes a note.*) Good.

**Helen** Funny you should mention it today –

**Manders** It's been playing on my mind.

**Helen** Because we almost had a fire there yesterday.

**Manders** You what?

**Helen** False alarm. Some wood shavings caught alight in the carpenter's workshop.

**Manders** Engstrand?

**Helen** Engstrand. I'm told he's often careless with his matches.

**Manders** He carries a fair few cares on his shoulders, I know –

**Helen** I'm sure.

**Manders** But tries to keep himself on the straight and narrow these days, thank God.

**Helen** Does he, who told you that?

**Manders** He told me himself.

**Helen** Oh.

**Manders** He's a good worker.

**Helen** When he's sober.

**Manders** Yes there is that. It's his leg, he said to me, he said he drinks to take away the pain . . .
    If you'd seen him, Helen . . . Look at me, I've almost a tear in my eye when I think of him so . . . grateful, he was, coming back to see me. That I'd got him the job out here, and close to his daughter . . .

**Helen** Well, he doesn't see much of her.

**Manders** No he speaks to her most days, he said.

**Helen** Oh, right.

**Manders** She's what he needs, you know. A hand of . . . restraint, and . . . and kindness.
That's the beauty of a man like Jacob Engstrand, to be so . . . open and vulnerable, and . . . and he blames himself, I know he does. He's the first to admit the mistakes he's made, and . . . But when he spoke to me in town, Helen, it led to me think, I think . . . if . . . for Regine, if it were at all possible –

**Helen** What about Regine?

**Manders** 'What about Regine'? –

**Helen** Her place is here, and at the children's home.

**Manders** He is her father, Helen.

**Helen** I know what kind of a father he's been to her.
No she won't be going back to him, not if I can help it.

**Manders** Now – Okay.
It's a sadness, I have to say, to see the man misjudged –

**Helen** I'm sorry it makes you sad but that's that.
Regine was brought up here and this is where she will stay.

**Manders** You seem almost . . . frightened –

**Helen** (*her face brightening*) Listen.
Osvald's coming down, that's enough of all that.

*Osvald enters. Stops when he sees them.*

**Osvald** Ah! Morning all. Or is it afternoon?

**Helen** Come here, darling.

**Osvald** Pastor Manders.

**Manders** My goodness.

**Osvald** Yes. Yep. The er . . . prodigal son. Just returned.

**Manders** And so he has.

**Helen** Ossie still remembers you weren't too keen on him going into painting, Pastor.

**Manders** Well, I stand corrected.
Welcome home, Osvald. You don't mind if I call you Osvald?

**Osvald** What else would you want to call me?

**Manders** Yes. Yes.
I'm not a complete . . . philistine by the way, I'm not a part of the . . . 'anti-art' brigade, who could be, I just think it's important for a man to be an artist but to still . . . keep a hold of himself.
As I'm sure many can.

**Osvald** We can only hope.

**Helen** Osvald's kept a firm hold of himself, just look at him.

**Osvald** Alright, Mother.

**Manders** I've seen your name in print a good few times, I've seen bright things.
Not so much lately, but still.

**Osvald** I haven't been working much just lately.

**Helen** Even an artist needs some rest.

**Manders** Of course. To recuperate and prepare no doubt for some great . . .
Painting.

**Osvald** Mother, when's lunch?

**Helen** In half an hour, darling. He still has an appetite, thank God.

**Manders** He likes a smoke, too. From a pipe, no less.

**Osvald** This belonged to my father, Pastor.

**Helen** Did it?

**Osvald** Found it upstairs.

**Manders** Yes. That's it.

**Helen** That's what?

**Manders** Osvald, in the doorway there with the pipe in his gob, I could have sworn he was his father, he's the spit of him.

**Osvald** Oh yeah?

**Helen** No.

**Manders** There is something in the mouth, is it in the lips, I don't know. Something he owes to the Captain, I'd say. When he's smoking anyway.

**Helen** Rubbish. He has a lovely mouth.

**Manders** Well, as did the Captain. Some would say.

**Osvald** Would they?

**Helen** Put the pipe away, Ossie, please I don't want smoke in here.

**Osvald** Not the first time I've had a go on this.

**Helen** I'm sure.

**Osvald** I was what – four? Five? Quick developer.

**Manders** Right.

**Helen** What do you mean?

**Osvald** You don't remember this?

**Helen** I'd like to think I'd remember a / thing –

**Osvald** I was mooching about upstairs one night, I dunno, I was waiting for dinner I guess, and who do I find, but Captain Daddy-o.

Up in his room, getting his big old smoke on up there, now – I think it's fair to say he'd probably had a few. And probably a few too many it's fair to say, but . . .

He puts me up on his knee, pipe in hand.

He says, 'There you go my son, you have a pipe on this pipe like a little big man.'

*Manders laughs, uncomfortably.*

**Helen** And he gave you his pipe?

**Osvald** Now people might say – and they'd be right, probably, to say that five years old is an early start to a tobacco-smoking life, but –

**Helen** I think you've dreamt this up –

**Osvald** No.

Father never bothered himself with . . . norms or . . . societal whatever-you-wanna-call-it, codes . . .

He did what the moment told him to do and served society all the better for it, the Pastor knows what I'm talking about, I think.

**Manders** I, recall . . .

**Osvald** A natural warmth that . . . made anything natural.

**Helen** And what happened then?

**Osvald** When?

**Helen** Well, with this pipe in your mouth, at four years old –

**Osvald** Oh then.
Well, I took in one big gulp.
And then I threw up on his shoes.

**Helen** Oh, Ossie.

**Osvald** And he laughed. I think I laughed.

**Helen** You can't remember that far back anyhow.

**Osvald** You were crying, Mother, when you the saw the state of me.

**Manders** The Captain was always the joker.

**Osvald** The Captain. Eccentric, true, and God love him for it, he put his name to some good and useful things around this dark old place . . . and never lived to see the fruits.

**Manders** You're in big shoes, Osvald.

**Osvald** (*in agreement*) You know?

**Manders** You should take it as inspiration now, to walk in them.

**Osvald** When the time comes.

**Manders** You'll be pleased, any rate, to be here for him tomorrow.

**Osvald** I am.

**Helen** And then I get to keep him for so long and that's the nicest thing of all.

**Manders** Up for the whole winter?

**Osvald** Maybe longer. It's good to be home.

**Helen**  Isn't it just?

**Manders**  You went out early into the world.

**Osvald**  Too early I think, sometimes.

**Helen**  Oh, what are you talking about, it does a bright boy good. Especially an only child. Can't be kept at home, and spoilt. By too much Mummy and Daddy.

**Manders**  Well, I think there are those who would question that, Mrs Alving. What better place is there for a child than at home?

**Osvald**  I'm with the Pastor there.

**Manders**  Take your own boy here. Shall we talk about him to his face? I don't think he's shy.
    You sent him off, and what then? What have the consequences been for young Oswald, a man of twenty-seven who's never known a proper home.

**Osvald**  Well – whoa – okay, that's – Hmm.

**Manders**  Well, I thought since you were young you'd moved mostly in artistic . . . circles.

**Osvald**  'Artistic . . . circles', er, yes, yes that's true.

**Manders**  And mostly with younger artists.

**Osvald**  Sometimes.

**Manders**  And most of these people – stop me if I'm wrong – I thought that most of these people . . . couldn't afford to marry or . . . or have a home, or family.

**Osvald**  That is true, of a lot of them, yes.

**Manders**  Whereas you, are a son of these shores, Oswald. There's a life here waiting for you.

**Osvald**  Yep.

**Manders**  The time comes, to . . . put away childish things.

**Osvald**  Childish?

**Manders**  You know what I mean.

**Osvald**  Yes, I think I do.

**Helen**  Ossie.

**Osvald**  But what's childish, I wonder, about . . . going out into the world, without a parent's hand, and . . . pursuing something. Something bigger than yourself.

**Manders**  There's something for you here that's . . . bigger than yourself alright, it's called a legacy.

**Osvald**  Uh-huh.

**Manders**  It's called community.

**Osvald**  Those are important things.

**Manders**  They are.

**Osvald**  But sometimes I think I just can't be bothered with them.

**Helen**  Osvald.

**Osvald**  This place is a job, anyone can do it.

**Manders**  But a family –

**Osvald**  Yeah, maybe I'll have one of those, one day. But not out here. I want to do what I want to do.

**Manders**  (*to Helen*) Do you see what I mean?

**Osvald**  'Childish things', d'you know, Pastor, when I've been living abroad these last few years, on some occasions a father would arrive.
A middle-aged feller, from a district just like this one.

**Manders**  Would they.

**Osvald** They'd come down, into our little artistic circle, to visit a son or a daughter, and to have a look around.

We'd sit together in tastefully humble drinking establishments, and as the atmosphere relaxed . . . the father among us would undo the top two buttons of his shirt . . . and a childish glint would appear in his eye, as out would come . . . stories.

Oh, debauchery and endeavour, Pastor Manders, their stories pissed all over ours.

**Manders** Fascinating, I'm sure –

**Osvald** They managed it, God love them. Before . . . duty and responsibility caught up with them, a carefree life.

And it was fucking wasted on them.

**Helen** Calm down, Ossie, it's not good for you.

**Osvald** The Pastor's worn me out.

Take a little walk before lunch. Get my strength back.

*He clutches his head.*

This tiredness again.

Forgive me, Pastor Manders, it . . . catches me like this sometimes . . . Excuse me.

*He exits.*

**Helen** Poor boy.

**Manders** Well, that's one way of putting it.

The prodigal son. His words.

*Helen is staring at him.*

And so then, what? What do you make of all this?

**Helen** I think he spoke the truth.

**Manders** Truth? In a load of . . . infantile posturing, the boy has no sense of principle!

34

**Helen** I often think over things, here on my own, things I wish I'd done quite differently, not done at all.

But I never dared say.

Now Osvald will speak for me.

**Manders** What's happened to you?

Talk to me, Helen. And think of me not as your business adviser, or . . . friend of the Captain but . . . but as *your* friend.

As the one you ran to, Helen, as the man of the cloth. Who stood before you in your darkest hour.

**Helen** Oh, and what does the man of the cloth have to say to me now?

**Manders** Well, first, he would like to jog your memory. And not a bad moment to do so – ten years, isn't it now, since your husband's passing, and tomorrow his memorial unveiled. And so then, tomorrow, I will speak to the world, so to speak.

But today I will speak to you alone –

**Helen** Then would you mind spitting it out? So to speak?

**Manders** You'd been married barely a year, you walked away, you ran. And refused to return.

**Helen** I was a deeply unhappy young girl, Pastor, yes.

**Manders** And people have a right, do they, to be happy?

Or is there something that comes first, is there something we might call – responsibility?

**Helen** Captain Alving had that a little confused. As I think you know.

**Manders** I heard the gossip, Helen, of course I did. I'm far from condoning the . . . the youthful excesses of your husband, but who am I to start casting stones?

And who – it isn't fashionable to say this I know, but who is a wife to sit in judgement of her husband?

Your duty was to bear your *cross*, Helen, I use the word without embarrassment. A cross bestowed on you by a higher authority, and you cast it off.

Where you should have been a . . . support and a guidance for a faltering man, you abandoned him. Risking your own good name, and . . . and coming quite close, pretty close you came to the names of others.

**Helen**  One other, I think you're talking about.

**Manders**  It was reckless, Helen, to come to my door.

**Helen**  Reckless? To a man of the cloth, and a friend, in my darkest hour?

**Manders**  You should thank God . . . God . . .
Be thankful I found the strength enough to not be . . . To be able to guide you, as I like to think I did, back to your home.

**Helen**  Yes, you certainly did that.

**Manders**  And wasn't it a blessing? And didn't Alving turn his back on whatever he was . . .
He lived with you and loved you, and my God, what a man of . . . enterprise, and charity for the whole area. Didn't he . . . allow you to . . . to bask in his own light, in sharing with you the work he was doing? I know he did.

Which leads me to my second point . . . to the second mistake I believe you have made.

**Helen**  What do you mean?

**Manders**  In the same way you ran from the duties of marriage, Helen, I ask you what about those of being a mother?

**Helen**  I beg your pardon?

**Manders** This . . . I mean what to call it, impulsiveness?
It seems to me you're happiest when . . . when running away and breaking things down and casting away all rules and restraints.

'I'm sick of being a wife, I'll move out. And I've had quite enough of my child, I'll give him to strangers to raise and be done with.'

**Helen** Yes, that's absolutely what I did, thank you, I see clearly now.

**Manders** The point I'm making –

**Helen** I sent him away for what's best for him.

**Manders** And now he's a stranger to you.

**Helen** He is not.

**Manders** Oh, come on.
And look how you've brought him back to you.
The children's home, you must know deep down . . .
You did your husband wrong, Helen, and now you build it in his memory.
Which is a wonderful thing.
But it's Oswald you must see to now.
His place is here, his father's legacy.
See him back to himself and away from this . . . selfish . . . perverse idea of what life is. If you just stand by, then . . . then you will stay guilty, Helen.
I'd be no friend to you or to God if I'd not told you straight.

*Silence.*

**Helen** Well, you've spoken, Pastor, and tomorrow you'll speak again, in my husband's memory.
I won't speak tomorrow.
But I'd like to share a few things with you now, if you don't mind.

**Manders**  You . . . must take some time, if you need, to consider what I've said, before –

**Helen**  No, I think I'll talk with you now, Pastor, please.
Everything you've said about my husband and our happy life together.
I'm surprised you can be so . . . candid, about a situation . . . about something you were quite absent from.
You were a regular guest in our home before you led me back to my 'duty' as you called it. Having done that you disappeared.

**Manders**  You moved away from town.

**Helen**  We did. But not so far as you couldn't have . . . stopped by, once in a while, It was only the children's home that brought you back here.

**Manders**  Helen if this, is a kind of . . . reproach, then . . . then for goodness sake remember –

**Helen**  Remember your position, yes. Your name. Your duties. One can never be careful enough with these reckless women –

**Manders**  That is not what I meant and you know it.

**Helen**  Alright.

**Manders**  I have cared, deeply for you –

**Helen**  Well, if that's what you've done then –
Then I'd like you to know a few things, and I'd like to tell you the truth.

**Manders**  And . . . and what is the truth?

**Helen**  What was the word, I thought it might appeal to you.
Dissolute.
My husband died as dissolute as he lived.

**Manders**  Dissolute.

**Helen**  And that is the truth.

**Manders**  Helen –

**Helen**  Nineteen years, and no . . . cure –

**Manders**  You'd best tell me what you mean by dissolute –

**Helen**  I mean he was an adulterer and a drunk. I mean he was the same as he ever was, and you sent me back to him. There was no . . . miraculous intervention from your friend up there or from anyone else, I went to *you*, for an intervention. But there was none forthcoming.

*A slight pause.*

**Manders**  And you're telling me *now* . . . You're telling me your whole life together was –

**Helen**  Was simultaneous with all the other lives that Alving led, so many at once. It was . . . an addiction, the psychologist called it.

**Manders**  Psychologist?

**Helen**  And life in here was a battle. Not between me and Alving, no, not so much that. But for Osvald.
To stop him knowing the man his father really was.
To stop the world knowing, this . . . fickle world, you know what Alving was to people, his charms –

**Manders**  Good . . . Christ –

**Helen**  And that isn't the end of it, that wasn't the end of it. Oh . . .
No, the worse of it happened here. Within our own four walls.

**Manders**  What happened here?

**Helen** Well not exactly here. In the dining room, actually.

I was . . . pottering about through there, I noticed the door was slightly ajar, I noticed Joanna. She was one of our staff here at the time, you might remember, nice enough girl. I came in from the garden with the . . . water for the flowers in there.

And then I heard Captain Alving's voice.

I heard him speak to her.

And she said – my God I can still hear it now –

'Let me go, Captain,' she said. 'Get away from me. Get off me.'

**Manders** I can't believe it.

I mean . . . My God, I knew . . . of course I realised . . . in his past –

**Helen** You knew nothing. I soon got to know everything. Oh yes, it was more than a little something, he had his way with her and there were consequences, I'm afraid.

**Manders** Consequences?

**Helen** I've tried my best for her.

Osvald . . . might be pleased to have a sister, I suppose.

**Manders** And this in the family home?

**Helen** Yes, quite. There's been more than one family made in this home. And that was one more than I could handle. I swore, then, that I would take some kind of control.

I sent Oswald abroad, and Alving didn't dare say anything.

Ossie had started to notice things, ask questions, I mean . . . as children do.

And so I lost him.

I didn't want him so much as breathing the air of this so-called . . . home.

I lost him.

And never had him back here as long as Alving lived.
No one has known the cost of all this for me.

**Manders** Helen, you have suffered.

**Helen** In the meantime I became Alving's nurse . . .
geisha . . . caretaker, I don't know. Occasionally I caught
him at it, Pastor.

**Manders** You . . . ?

**Helen** Came home to him on the kitchen table there,
with whoever she was that month.

**Manders** Oh . . .

**Helen** And then after I sit and watch him drink. A
regular audience, for his . . . rambling inanities. It was
all I could to do keep him in the house of a night.
    And all of these wonderful projects to his name, this
man who I had drag to bed each night, when he was
finally comatose?
    Do you think he was capable of all that alone?
    On his good days I spurred him on.
    And on his bad ones, I carried his whole weight.

**Manders** And you're dedicating a home to this man,
a home for children?

**Helen** Oh well, that's a guilty conscience, isn't it, Pastor?
    I could hear your voice in my head all those years.
Telling me of my responsibilities.
    I was terrified the truth would get out one day, I
thought an orphanage would be the sort of thing that
would . . . reassure people.
    And there's another reason.
    I don't want my boy to inherit a single penny from
that man.
    I wanted that money all spent.

**Manders** So it's all Alving's money that's –

**Helen** I've worked it out very carefully. Year on year I've set up to donate the exact amount the late Captain brings to me.

**Manders** Right.

**Helen** I don't want a penny of Alving's money in Osvald's hands. Everything he'll have from me, I swear it.

*Osvald enters. He has left his hat and jacket outside.*

Are you back with us again, my darling boy?

**Osvald** Well, the rain is bringing a kind of 'close all the doors and windows' vibe, but – it's lunchtime. Thank the Lord.

**Regine** (*entering from the dining room, with parcel*) This package arrived for you, Mrs Alving.

**Helen** (*to Manders*) These'll be the songs for tomorrow.

**Manders** What? Yes.

**Regine** And lunch is ready.

**Helen** Thank you, Regine. (*With the parcel.*) I just want to have a look at these.

**Regine** (*to Osvald*) Red or white, for Mr Alving?

**Osvald** Both, for Mr Alving.

**Regine** Très bien.

*She exits to the dining room. A slight pause.*

**Osvald** Think I might . . . help open the bottles.

*He exits to the dining room.*

**Helen** (*having opened the parcel*) Yes, look at them, here they are. Good.

**Manders**  How in God's name I'll come out with . . . a speech, tomorrow, I –

**Helen**  You'll manage.
And then after tomorrow this whole thing'll be over.
It'll be as if that man had never lived in this house.
As if he'd never lived at all.
There'll be no one but a boy, and his mother.

*From the dining room can suddenly be heard a chair crashing to the ground, simultaneous with –*

**Regine**  (*sharp, but whispering*) Osvald! Are you mad?!
Let go of me!

*Helen starts in terror.*

**Helen**  Oh –!

*She stares at Manders, who holds her gaze. Then stares with horror towards the dining-room door.*

**Manders**  Is that –?
Was that –?

**Helen**  Ghosts. Returning, Pastor Manders.
They're in the dining room again.

*Manders is staring at her.*

**Manders**  But . . .
Regine is –

**Helen**  Don't say a word.
Come with me.

*She moves towards the dining-room door, and Pastor Manders follows.*

# Act Two

*The same room.*

*Damp fog still lying heavy across the landscape.*
*Pastor Manders and Helen enter from the dining*
*room.*

**Helen** Well, I hope you enjoyed that, Pastor.
(*Speaking through doorway.*) Are you joining us,
Ossie?

**Osvald** (*off*) No, I'll head out for a bit.

**Helen** Yes, why don't you, I think the rain's held off for
now.

*She closes the dining-room door and calls out to the*
*hall.*

Regine?

**Regine** (*entering*) Yes, Mrs Alving?

**Helen** Could you pop upstairs and give the plants in my
bedroom some water.

**Regine** Yes, will do.

*She exits. Helen checks that she has gone, then closes*
*the door.*

**Manders** He can't hear anything in there?

**Helen** Not with the door closed. Anyway, he's going out.

**Manders** I still can't get a hold of all this, Helen, I feel –
Trying to . . . eat one bite of that meal, I –

44

**Helen** Likewise.
But now what?

**Manders** Quite. God knows I try my best, but I don't know . . . In this kind of a situation, I –

**Helen** I don't think anything's happened between them yet.

**Manders** No. Well, God willing . . . We have to stop it.

**Helen** She's one of Osvald's little whims, no more than that, I'm sure of it.

**Manders** A little whim she may well be, but listen to how he spoke earlier. He wants to do anything he wants –

**Helen** She has to leave the house.

**Manders** Yes.

**Helen** But where can she go?

**Manders** Well, to her father, Helen.

**Helen** To who, did you say?

**Manders** To –
But Engstrand isn't . . .
Oh, this can't be possible.
Are you sure –

**Helen** Yes I am sure. I wish I weren't.
Joanna left us straight away. With a not insubstantial sum to see her through.
She must have known Engstrand previously, she got to know him again.
Made a certain amount of noise, no doubt, about the money she'd fallen into and about the foreigner, that was it, the Englishman she'd been with who'd so sadly failed to sail back into town aboard his yacht that summer.

Then very quickly they were married. Well, you married them yourself.

**Manders**  The man who came to see me then . . . was a wreck, Helen.
And so full of remorse, for a life he said he'd not lived well, and that now he'd got his girl pregnant and he was committed, he said, to doing right by them both, and what a fool he'd been for not . . . taking things slowly, he said –

**Helen**  He said what he had to say.

**Manders**  The lies he told!
And for how much?
How much was this girl given?

**Helen**  Three hundred kronar.

**Manders**  Three hundred kronar he takes. For a marriage built on a lie.

**Helen**  And wasn't my marriage a lie?

**Manders**  But that was an utterly different circumstance –

**Helen**  Was it? I don't think so. The price was different, that's true.

**Manders**  You had looked into your heart, Helen.

**Helen**  My heart was in a different place altogether, I think you know it was.
It was with someone else.

**Manders**  (*distant*) If I had known . . .
If that had been made plain to me I would never have come here. As a guest in your husband's house.

**Helen**  My mother was overjoyed at the prospect, a captain no less, my God. If she could see it all now.

**Manders** No one could have foreseen how things have happened, the point remains . . .

You entered into a marriage according to God's own law.

**Helen** It's God and his laws I'm starting to think are behind all the misery in this world.

**Manders** That is a sinful thing to say.

A sad thing.

**Helen** Sinful it may be, but not sad.

I can't . . . live to the tune of these laws any longer, I want to be free.

I should have . . . had it out in the open years ago, I was a coward –

**Manders** A coward?

**Helen** They could have said, 'Oh, the poor man deserves a bit of fun, I mean, his own wife upped sticks and left him –'

**Manders** They'd have been within their rights, to have said that, if that was –

**Helen** If I was the woman I should have been I'd have taken Osvald and said to him, 'My darling boy, your father doesn't love you, he loves the drink, and he loves all women but me –'

**Manders** Helen . . . I'm beginning to think –

**Helen** Yes, I'm beginning to think as well, and it's all too late!

**Manders** Cowardice, you're calling it?!

**Helen** Was I brave?

**Manders** 'Honour thy mother and father', the child is told, now how was Osvald to have done that if he'd known . . .

**Helen** The truth?

Yes, God protect us from knowing the truth.

**Manders** The truth that Osvald knows is that his father was a great and loving man, and I know, Helen, that you made no attempt at having him know otherwise.

All those letters you sent. From a happy home.

**Helen** Yes, I lied to him year after year.

**Manders** He took pride in the picture you painted, Helen. Now you can take pride in that.

**Helen** Perhaps.

But what I can't have now is him and Regine. I won't have her hurt.

**Manders** God forbid.

**Helen** If I knew . . .

If one had a sense that it were serious, and they'd be happy together –

**Manders** What do you mean?

**Helen** I don't know, Regine's not the settling type, that's the feeling I get.

**Manders** And what if she was?

**Helen** If I weren't so pathetic I'd say to him 'Marry her! Have it any way you like, but no more lies!'

**Manders** The idea of those two . . .

**Helen** But I won't allow it, that's what I've said.

**Manders** Because you're pathetic, you said, yes.

Point being if you weren't so pathetic, then . . . then God only knows what parody of a relationship you'd happily give your blessing –

**Helen**  It was a relationship like that which led to all of us, the Bible says, is that not right, Pastor?

**Manders**  This is hardly the time for that discussion. With a woman who calls it cowardice, to have lived by natural law –

**Helen**  Oh, let me clarify it, Pastor, cowardice hardly covers it. I am petrified.
I'm haunted by ghosts.
And I think I'll never be free of them.

**Manders**  You feel . . . haunted . . .

**Helen**  Well, ghosts isn't quite the word . . . all clanking chains and skeletal fingers, they're fresh-faced, the things I'm talking about, they never grow old.
My Osvald, and Regine just now, I almost thought they were ghosts.

**Manders**  But what do you / mean –

**Helen**  But then I've a feeling we all are, Pastor, all ghosts. Not just of our mothers and fathers, and their mothers and fathers before them, but . . . inside us it's . . . all the dead beliefs and opinions they held, we think we've outgrown them . . .
I don't know, I read a newspaper, for what's it worth, I can see ghosts, creeping out from between the lines . . .
The whole country's full of them.
The whole world.
Holding our hands, from the moment we're born.
And they never let go.

**Manders**  That is a cynical . . . an ungodly way of thinking –

**Helen**  You're the one who made me think.
Who forced me to embrace in the name of . . . duty everything my mind rebelled against and called wrong.

49

That's when I started unpicking, the seams of your learning.

A simple cloth it appeared at first.

But then I pushed deeper and deeper into the fabric.

And found it was machine-woven.

**Manders** (*quiet, shaken*) And this is what I get?

In return for the hardest battle of my life?

**Helen** A sad defeat, I'd call it.

**Manders** I . . . struggled against myself, Helen, and I overcame.

**Helen** It was a crime against the both of us.

**Manders** When you came to me distraught.

And said to me, 'Here I am, here, come and take me,' and I said, 'Go back, to your lawful wedded husband,' and that was a crime?

**Helen** I think so.

**Manders** We don't understand one another.

**Helen** Not any more.

**Manders** I, am a decent man, in a world . . .

Never did I think of you as anything other than another man's wife.

**Helen** The memory sometimes cheats, I think. We forget what we were like, how we change.

**Manders** I am the same as I always was.

**Helen** Oh, yes, yes, alright. Enough of the olden days.

You're up to your eyes in people and their problems. And I'm out here. Fighting ghosts, inside and out.

**Manders** And I will help you.

After what you've said today I can't . . .

I won't see a girl like Regine be kept in this house.

**Helen** Well, shouldn't we do something for her –

**Manders** For now she should be with her father, and
that's –
   But Engstrand isn't her . . .
   That he kept such a secret from me, I should –

*A knock on the hallway door.*

**Helen** Who's that? Come in?

*Engstrand begins to enter, dressed smartly.*

Engstrand?

*Manders laughs to himself in disbelief.*

**Engstrand** Hope I'm not interrupting, there was no one
about, to let me in the right way, so I've said to meself:
'Jacob. You take the plunge mate, and –'

*He knocks.*

'Give 'em a knock.' As I did.

**Helen** What can I do for you?

**Engstrand** Erm. Begging your pardon, sort of thing, but it
was the Pastor, I was hoping to have a quick chat with –

**Manders** What about?

**Engstrand** Pastor Manders.
   Erm.
   Well what I was wanting to say is . . . All of us down
there have been paid now – Nice one, Mrs A . . . much
appreciated –

**Manders** What is it, Engstrand?

**Engstrand** And so, what with everything finished off,
I thought it might be nice . . . considering how we all
worked so well together and that, I thought how about
we round it all off with a little blessing? In the orphanage. I
mean the children's home, tonight.

**Manders**  A blessing.

**Engstrand**  Usually say a few prayers down there meself, end of the day.

**Helen**  Do you really, Mr Engstrand?

**Engstrand**  Every now and again.
  Ask for a bit of . . . support.
  But I mean the way I do it's not the same as the Pastor does, I know . . .
  I'm a humble man, me, I'm . . .
  But I thought . . . seeing as you're here –

**Manders**  Jacob, I must ask you something.

**Engstrand**  Oh yeah?

**Manders**  Do you think . . . that you are in the right frame of mind, for a blessing?
  I mean is your conscience . . . in the right condition?

**Engstrand**  Conscience?
  Slow down, it's . . . it's neither the time or place for going down that road –

**Manders**  It is the exact time and place I'm afraid. What do you think?

**Engstrand**  Well, conscience, is . . . It's . . . it's a nasty old thing, it can be that, sometimes –

**Manders**  You'd admit that much, well that's a start.
  Tell me then. About Regine.

**Engstrand**  What about Regine?

**Manders**  Don't –

**Helen**  Pastor Manders.

**Manders**  I will speak to him.

**Engstrand**  Gimme the horrors, look at me like that.
  What . . . what's the matter with our Regine?

**Manders**  Nothing as yet, we hope.
Or is there?
You are her father.
Or aren't you?

**Engstrand**  Someone's spilt the beans about me and Joanna.

**Manders**  No more lies. Joanna told Mrs Alving everything, before she left this house.

**Engstrand**  She did what?

**Manders**  You're found out, Engstrand.

**Engstrand**  She fucking –
She swore to God, Pastor!

**Manders**  To God?

**Engstrand**  Well . . . She promised me!

**Manders**  All these years you've been lying to me, Engstrand. To someone who's only had total faith in you.
Haven't I been there for you with advice, and acted in any way I could to be of benefit to you, always. Haven't I?

**Engstrand**  You've had me back, untold occasions, yes.

**Manders**  And this is the thanks I get?
I've put myself on the line . . . umpteen times for you, when others were minded to leave you out to dry.

**Engstrand**  I know.

**Manders**  And through every year that's passed you have owed me the truth, and not given it, and so where do we go from here?
Nowhere, I'm afraid, Jacob, is the way I see it.

**Engstrand**  Fair play, Pastor.
I've no sob story . . . to try and justify meself, I'll hold me peace.

**Manders** Right.

*A slight pause.*

**Engstrand** Although one thing I would say . . . Looking at it from Joanna's . . . p.o.v., I mean . . .
Should she have gone blabbing? I mean the truth about herself?
What good would that have done anyone?
I mean if you put yourself in her shoes –

**Manders** In her shoes?

**Engstrand** Alright – Forgetting Joanna –
What I'm trying to say is, if you yourself, Pastor, had . . . strayed, so to speak. And strayed towards doing summat to be ashamed of, in the eyes of some, well . . . Should we be judging a . . . a weak woman . . . so harshly?

**Manders** I am not judging the woman. I blame you.

**Engstrand** Could I ask the Pastor a tiny question?

**Manders** Try me.

**Engstrand** Is it right and proper . . . in the Bible, sort of thing, for a man to raise the fallen?

**Manders** In a manner of speaking, yes.

**Engstrand** And is it also right and proper for a man to keep his word?

**Manders** Absolutely it is. But –

**Engstrand** When Joanna had been taken advantage of by this Englishman or . . . or American or Russian or whatever he was, she came back to town . . .
Now I'd tried it on with her a couple of times in the past, but she was a pretty young thing she was, and –
Well. This leg. She was having none of it.

I told you, didn't I, in a dance that time, a filthy, degenerate place full of the worst kind of seafaring man, and as I was giving it the spiel about the Good Lord's work –

**Helen** (*listening, at the window*) Oh God.

**Manders** They threw you down the stairs, Engstrand, yes. You carry your wounds with honour.

**Engstrand** But the thing was, with Joanna back in town . . . I mean the state of her, Pastor, when she came to see me, crying and . . . in absolute bits she was, and I felt sorry for her, I did.

**Manders** And so?

**Engstrand** And so I said to her.
This American, slash Englishman, slash Russian. Well he's out on the seven seas now.
And you, Joanna, are left behind.
A little angel.
A little fallen angel.
But Jacob Engstrand can stand on his own two feet.
Metaphorically speaking.

**Manders** Go on.

**Engstrand** And then I took her in my arms and I married her, and . . . so the world'd never know she'd got busy with a foreigner and, and –
So yeah.

**Manders** It's a story to tell, Engstrand, and you come out of it with some dignity, but the part you miss is that you took money from this woman.

**Engstrand** Money? No, not a single penny, mate.

*Manders looks at Helen.*

**Manders** But . . .

**Engstrand** Hang on.

It's very foggy this, but I do remember . . .

Yes.

Joanna had a few quid knocking about.

But I told her where to stick it, you know.

I've gone – 'Mammon', you know, 'the flippin' . . . the wages of sin, the filthy gold or notes or whatever it was, we chuck that back in the face of the American. Russian. Englishman.'

Who, by that time had . . . Well he'd sailed away.

Then me and Joanna agreed, we'd put the money towards the baby, and raising her up with it.

And we did, I can swear to that, I can trace every penny.

**Manders** If this is true, then . . .

Then it does make us see things differently.

**Engstrand** I hope so, Pastor.

I've tried me best, I have, for Regine, to be a real father to her, but . . .

I am a weak man, I'm afraid to say . . .

**Manders** Jacob.

**Engstrand** Well, I did what I could, and I made a go of it with Joanna, God rest her. I think we did alright.

Never crossed me mind, any rate, that I should . . . go blagging to the Pastor about . . . how I'd also done a good deed in this world.

That's not Jacob Engstrand's way, I'm a humble man. I'm a weak man, Pastor. And weakness I've come to talk to you about, more often than I'd like, fair play, I'll admit that.

And you ask me about me conscience . . .

Like I say . . .

It's a nasty one . . .

**Manders** Jacob Engstrand, give me your hand.

**Engstrand** Well . . .

**Manders** No buts.

*He shakes Engstrand's hand.*

There we are.

**Engstrand** And . . . as a humble man . . . to ask your forgiveness –

**Manders** I am the one, to be asking forgiveness of you.

**Engstrand** Oh . . . don't think you got that right.

**Manders** I'm sorry, Jacob.
I misjudged you.
And if there was something I could do, as a way of expressing my regret, and my goodwill towards you –

**Engstrand** Oh yeah?

**Manders** Then I will gladly oblige.

**Engstrand** Well now you mention it, there is something I've got in the mix back in town, it's a . . . a cultural centre.

**Manders** Really.

**Engstrand** With an eye for, you know, the passing trade, the sailors and the seafaring types, don't knock their appetite for . . . for culture, and . . . music and . . . possibly dance –

**Manders** It sounds very intriguing, Jacob, and do you know what I'm thinking now?

**Engstrand** What's that?

**Manders** That blessing you were talking about – why don't we go down to the chapel and see to that? And afterwards we can talk some more.

**Engstrand** But it won't take a sec, just to give you the specs and –

No – No, the blessing, let's have the blessing first –

**Manders** You go and light some candles and make the place ready.

**Engstrand** Alright, Pastor.
(*To Helen, a farewell.*) Mrs Alving. (*He stops.*) Take good care of Regine for me. (*Wipes a tear from his eye.*) I don't mind telling you, Mrs A, the child of Joanna and God knows who she may be, but . . .

She's taken a piece of my heart, that girl.

*He excuses himself, and exits.*

**Manders** Well, what do you reckon, Mrs Alving?
There's a different take on the matter.

**Helen** A different take, yes.

**Manders** A little lesson. For me, anyway. As to how cautious we should be about judging someone in . . . haste.

But what a joy it is, also, to find yourself sometimes . . . happily mistaken.

Or what do you think?

**Helen** I think you're an overgrown child, Pastor Manders, and always will be.
(*Putting her hands on his shoulders.*) And I want to throw my arms around you.

**Manders** (*freeing himself*) Helen, what have we said –

**Helen** Oh, please don't be frightened of me –

**Manders** Keep a hold of yourself.

*He begins sorting together the documents.*

I'll put the documents together.

*He finishes.*

Right. I'll leave you be. Keep an eye on Osvald when he comes in.
 I'll be back later, Helen.

*He exits.*
 *Helen sighs, and looks out of the window for a moment. She tidies up a little, then moves towards the dining room, but stops in the doorway with a small cry.*

**Helen** Osvald, are you still here?

**Osvald** (*in dining room*) Finishing off my cigar, Mama.

**Helen** I thought you'd gone out ages ago.

**Osvald** In this weather?

*A glass clinks. Helen lets the door remain open and sits down with her knitting on the sofa by the window.*

Was that Pastor Manders who left just now?

**Helen** Yes, he went down to the home.

**Osvald** Mm-hmm. (*Glass and decanter clink again.*)

**Helen** Oh, Ossie, be careful with that, it's very strong.

**Osvald** Good for the damp.

**Helen** Don't you want to sit in here with me?

**Osvald** I thought I can't smoke in there.

**Helen** Oh, you can have a cigar.

**Osvald** Oh yeah? Just a little drop more'll do the trick. There.

*He comes in, with his cigar, and closes the door behind him. Brief silence.*

Where did Manders go?

**Helen** I told you, he went to the children's home.

**Osvald** Oh yeah. Good for him.

**Helen** You shouldn't have sat on your own so long.

**Osvald** It was cosy, Mummy. (*He cuddles her.*) I'm just a boy who's come home . . . To sit at his mother's table, and eat his mother's home cooking.

**Helen** Oh my Ossie.

**Osvald** I mean, what the fuck else can I do, I can't work –

**Helen** What do you mean?

**Osvald** In this . . . smudge they call daylight, how can anyone function out here?

**Helen** Oh, my poor boy, you know perhaps it wasn't a good idea for you to come back.

**Osvald** Well, I had to and I did.

**Helen** I'd sooner go without you here than seeing you so unhappy.

**Osvald** And it's such a joy is it, to see me home?

**Helen** How can you ask your own mother –

**Osvald** You've managed without me before.

**Helen** Managed, yes, I have. But that's not the same as living.

**Osvald** No it's not.

*Silence. Twilight begins to set in. Osvald paces the room. He has put the cigar down. He stops, and faces her.*

**Helen** What is it?

**Osvald** Can I sit with you?

**Helen** Of course you can.

**Osvald** Because there's something I have to say –

**Helen** Well, you can say anything you want –

**Osvald** Because I can't bear it any more.

**Helen** Osvald, what is it?

**Osvald** I couldn't write to you about it, and since I've been back I . . .

**Helen** Darling?

**Osvald** Yesterday I tried just . . . blanking it out, just . . . pushing the thoughts from my mind, but No. No, it's no use.

**Helen** (*standing*) Ossie, tell me the truth.

**Osvald** Sit down, Mother.
This tiredness I've been on about, from the journey.

**Helen** What about it?

**Osvald** Shush.
Because . . . what I'm talking about is not an ordinary . . . tiredness –

**Helen** (*wanting to stand*) Oh, tell me you're not ill.

**Osvald** Sit down. Just . . .
It's not an ordinary kind of illness, either.

*He clasps his head with his hands.*

Oh, I am . . . broken. Is the word for me.
Destroyed.
I'll never work again.

*He covers his face with his hands, and falls into her lap.*

**Helen** Osvald . . . Look at me . . .
This isn't true!

**Osvald** Can you imagine something as bad as that, can you imagine, to live and not to work, to be a zombie –

**Helen** Ossie, tell me what's happened.

**Osvald** I don't know. I don't know what's happened, I don't know how . . .
No matter what you think or what Manders thinks, I never lived . . . recklessly, I didn't sleep around, that wasn't me –

**Helen** But what do you mean? I'm sure you didn't.

**Osvald** But then how this?

**Helen** You must be completely exhausted, Osvald, that's all this is –

**Osvald** That's what I thought to begin with but no.
The last time I came. I had headaches. Yes?

**Helen** I don't know –

**Osvald** I went away again . . . They settled down, and then one morning . . .
Like a vice around my neck.

**Helen** And then what?

**Osvald** And then I thought, I hoped . . . Oh, when I was growing up I'd had pains, that came and went away again, but these . . . I couldn't *work*! I wanted to paint, I wanted to start a new project, but . . .
It was like the drive I'd had inside me had . . . evaporated. I couldn't concentrate, I felt dizzy, everything spinning. I . . . went to the doctor.

**Helen** And for God's sake what did he say?

**Osvald** I went to a very good doctor, Mother, at the top of his profession, he'd probably call himself, and he asked me a long list of interesting questions, none of which had one thing to do with anything and then . . . he told me.

**Helen** What?

**Osvald** He said to me – 'Vermoulu.'

**Helen** Well, what does that . . .

**Osvald** Worm-eaten, is the direct translation, not a bad one.
   Worm-eaten from birth, he said, and when I asked, as best I could, if he would mind elaborating, he said –
   (*Clenches his fist.*) Oh –!

**Helen** Osvald?

**Osvald** He said 'The sins of the father'.

**Helen** He said . . .

**Osvald** I wanted to hit him.

**Helen** 'The sins of the father'.

**Osvald** Are visited on the son, I think was the implication of this . . . churchgoing man of medicine.
   Obviously, I told him in no uncertain terms that my particular father was quite without . . . sin.
   He was a clean man, and had nothing to pass on down in that department, But even that wouldn't satisfy him, it wasn't until I'd sat down with him and your letters, can you imagine? And translated them as best I could –

**Helen** And what then?

**Osvald** And then what could he say?

He said, well then, if he'd been on the wrong track at first . . .

Then he told me it must have been me.

Not in so many words, but he told me it was the life I was leading, that I must have been in contact with people who . . .

That I'd brought it upon myself.

**Helen** Osvald, you mustn't think that –

**Osvald** What else is there to think? There's no cure!

To think . . . on the things I could have done . . . On the things I *should* have done, if I could go back and live it again then I would, but I can't.

*He collapses and buries his head in the sofa.*

If it was something inherited . . . beyond my control . . .

But to have wasted away my own happiness . . . my own health, to have done it myself!

**Helen** Ossie darling, I promise you . . . I promise you it can't be so bad –

**Osvald** You don't know.

And bringing all this to *you* . . .

I sometimes wish . . . you didn't love me as much as you do.

**Helen** My only boy! My only one in the world!

**Osvald** I know. And that's the hardest thing.

But now I've told you, and . . . let's not talk about it today any more.

I want a drink.

**Helen** What kind of a drink?

**Osvald** Anything, I'll finish the wine off from lunch.

**Helen** Osvald –

**Osvald** I need something, to wash away this . . .

*He goes into the conservatory.*

God, it's dark.

*Helen rings the bell for attention.*

And this rain. Week after week. I don't think I've seen a ray of sun all the times I've been back here.

**Helen** And now you're thinking about going away again –

**Osvald** I'm not thinking about anything.
I can't think.
I try not to.

**Regine** (*entering from the dining room*) Mrs Alving?

**Helen** Yes. Regine, let's bring the fire in here.

**Regine** Yes, of course.

*Helen moves towards Osvald.*

**Helen** Osvald, speak to me, don't pretend I'm not here –

**Osvald** I've told you . . . everything.

*Regine brings an electric heater over.*

**Helen** Thank you, Regine. And could you bring half a bottle of champagne?

**Regine** Yes, Mrs Alving.

*She exits.*

**Osvald** Very nice.

*He touches his mother's face.*

I knew Mother wouldn't let me go thirsty.

**Helen** You can have anything you want from now.

**Osvald**  Really?

**Helen**  Oh, my poor boy –

**Osvald**  Anything I want?

**Helen**  Osvald –

**Osvald**  Shh!

*Regine brings a tray with half a bottle of champagne and two glasses, which she places on the table.*

**Regine**  Would you like me to open –

**Osvald**  Thank you, Regine, I'll do it.

*Regine exits.*

**Helen**  What is it you want?

**Osvald**  (*busy with the bottle*) Let's have . . . a drink first. Or two.

*He is about to pour a second glass when she stops him.*

**Helen**  I don't want anything.

**Osvald**  All the more for me then.

*He empties the glass, re-fills it, empties that as well, then sits by the table.*

**Helen**  Ossie?

**Osvald**  (*without looking at her*) You and Manders, at lunchtime, what was going on there?

**Helen**  What do you mean?

**Osvald**  You seemed quiet, Mama, the both of you. Anyway, listen. What do you think of Regine?

**Helen**  Of Regine?

**Osvald** Yes.
She's a bit special, isn't she?

**Helen** Dear Ossie, I . . . I know Regine a little better than you –

**Osvald** Lucky you.

**Helen** She lived a difficult life, before she came here, I only wish I'd taken her in sooner –

**Osvald** Oh so do I. She is beautiful. Truly.

*He re-fills her glass.*

**Helen** Regine is not without . . . flaws –

**Osvald** 'Flaws'? Who isn't?

**Helen** I'm very fond of Regine, I'm responsible for her, I like to think, and if any harm should come to her –

**Osvald** No. No harm will come to her.
She'll save me.

**Helen** What on earth do you mean?

**Osvald** I can't do it alone.

**Helen** Ossie, your Mother is here –

**Osvald** I know she is, but life's unliveable here –

**Helen** Osvald –

**Osvald** And for you to watch me in this state . . . No, I want to get away.

**Helen** But when you're so ill –

**Osvald** If it was just the illness I would stay.
But it's everything else. The regret, this . . . constant, what is it, recrimination, and . . .
And the fear.

**Helen** What frightens you Osvald?

**Osvald** Oh, enough questions, I can't describe it.

*Helen rings for attention.*

What are you doing?

**Helen** I want my boy to be happy.
I don't want him sat here, his face like . . .

*Regine enters.*

More champagne. A whole bottle. Please.

**Regine** Yes.

*She exits.*

**Osvald** Mother.

**Helen** Do you think we don't know how to live out here?

**Osvald** My God, she is wonderful isn't she? That body, and that spirit.

**Helen** Oh, sit down, Ossie, please. Let's try and talk . . . .

**Osvald** I did Regine a little wrong, Mother, I need to put it right.

**Helen** What?

**Osvald** Last time I was home, she was asking me. About the world, about my travels . . . She has a fascination, with all things French, it's quite sweet really –

**Helen** And so?

**Osvald** And so I said to her – 'Paris. Shall we go?' And her eyes lit up. She said 'Really?'
I said 'Maybe one day.'
And then I forgot all about it.

And then yesterday, when I saw her again, I asked her if she was happy, I'd be staying so long, and she said . . .

**Helen** Osvald?

**Osvald** She gave me the saddest look, and said 'What about our trip to Paris?'

**Helen** Oh God.

**Osvald** She's even been learning French.

**Helen** That's why she wanted the lessons –

**Osvald** I saw this beautiful, healthy, sweet-natured woman in front of me – I mean someone I'd barely even noticed before –
But now stood there almost saying 'Come and take me', with her arms wide open.

**Helen** Osvald, please.

**Osvald** And suddenly it was obvious, it's her.
She's alive.
She could make me live again.

**Helen** She could save you, is that what you said, my darling boy –

*Regine enters from the dining room, with a bottle of champagne.*

**Regine** Sorry it took so long, I had to go to the cellar.

**Osvald** Another glass, Regine, please.

**Regine** Yes. Oh – er, Mrs Alving's glass is there –?

**Osvald** A glass for you, please, Regine.

*Regine starts and gives Helen a quick, shy sideways glance.*

Quickly please.

**Regine**  Mrs Alving?

**Helen**  Get the glass, Regine.

*Regine exits to the dining room.*

**Osvald**  The way she walks. So confident. So purposeful.

**Helen**  This isn't going to happen.

**Osvald**  It already has. There's nothing to argue about.

*Regine enters with an empty glass, which she keeps hold of.*

Sit down, Regine.

*Regine looks at Helen. She nods her permission.*
*Regine sits in the chair by the dining-room door, keeping hold of the glass.*

**Helen**  Osvald. You were talking about . . . being alive.

**Osvald**  Yes. In a deeper way than most people are out here.
I haven't seen much life around here, that's for sure. It's not that kind of a place.

**Helen**  And you don't feel alive when you're with me?

**Osvald**  Here? No.
It's . . . hard to understand –

**Helen**  I think I understand it now.

**Osvald**  You can be alive through work. It can give you meaning. But that doesn't happen here either.

**Helen**  Tell me more.

**Osvald**  People here are taught that life is a curse. A kind of . . . constant, pre-emptive punishment for sins they're too fucking scared to commit.

**Helen** A vale of tears, yes I remember that alright –

**Osvald** People don't believe all that in the real world
any more.
   People believe in choice, in life for life's sake.
   People call it out, that kind of teaching, for what it is.
   A slander, on the beautiful . . . simple practice of just
being alive.
   That's why I'm so . . . terrified of staying at home
with you.

**Helen** What are you scared of, here?

**Osvald** I'm scared that everything inside me will . . .
wither.

**Helen** You think that would happen?

**Osvald** I know it would. With you?
   I'm sorry, Mother.
   A place becomes a part of us.

**Helen** (*standing*) I can see it now.

**Osvald** What?

**Helen** Osvald, something's become quite clear to me . . .
   And now I can speak.

**Osvald** What do you mean?

**Regine** (*standing*) Perhaps I should leave you two –

**Helen** Stay here please, Regine, I want to speak to you
too.
   Osvald, Regine, I want you both to know the truth –

**Osvald** Manders is coming –

*Manders enters from the hall.*

**Manders** Ah. Glasses all round, is it?

**Regine** (*putting the glass down; French accent*) Pardon.

**Osvald** We're having a good discussion.

**Manders** Oh, likewise, I've had a very good discussion. With your father, Regine. We've prayed and talked together.

**Helen** Pastor Manders –

**Manders** There is a man, on a righteous path. I've said before he needs a hand to hold along the way. Regine, your place is with him.

**Regine** Thank you, Pastor, I think it's not.

**Manders** Now listen to me –

**Osvald** Regine is coming with me, Pastor.

**Manders** Is she now? Coming with you where?

**Osvald** Anywhere but here, I think. She'll be my wife, if she has to be. If she'll have me.

**Manders** Oh, God save us –

**Regine** This . . . was not known to me, Pastor.

**Osvald** Or if I stay here she stays with me.

**Regine** Here?!

**Manders** (*to Helen*) A good discussion you've had, is it?

**Helen** Neither will happen. I will speak now.

**Manders** You're not going to . . .?

**Helen** People will know the truth, and no one will suffer from it.

**Manders** Helen, no.

**Osvald** What are you talking about?

**Regine** Listen!
There's people shouting outside.

*She goes to the conservatory and looks out.*

**Osvald** What's happening? Where's the light coming from?

**Regine** The children's home is on fire!

**Manders** What are you talking about? I've just come from there!

**Osvald** Where's my jacket –

**Helen** No, Osvald, stay here –

**Osvald** That place is my father's!

*He runs out of the conservatory door.*

**Helen** Get my scarf, Regine! My God, it's completely ablaze!

**Manders** Of course it is! As a punishment on this house!

**Helen** Yes, Pastor. I'm sure you're absolutely right, as always. Come on, Regine.

*Helen and Regine hurry out through the hall, and Manders exits after them.*

# Act Three

*The same room. The lamp on the table is still lit.*
    *Dark outside, a faint glow of the fire in the background.*
    *Helen, her head covered by a scarf, is in the*
*conservatory looking out.*
    *Regine, also wearing a scarf, stands a little way behind*
*her.*

**Helen** All gone. Burnt to the ground.

**Regine** The basement's still burning.

**Helen** Why hasn't Ossie come back? There's nothing to save.

**Regine** Shall I go down with his jacket?

**Helen** He hasn't even his jacket on him?

**Regine** It's hanging up in the hall.

**Helen** Oh, he must be back by now, I'll go and find him.

    *She exits via the garden door.*

**Manders** (*entering from the hall*) Is Mrs Alving here?

**Regine** She went out to the garden.

**Manders** This is the worst night of my life, Regine.

**Regine** It's awful.

**Manders** Oh . . . It's beyond anything, it's . . .

**Regine** What could have started it?

**Manders** I don't know.

*He looks at her.*

Don't tell me you, as well as your . . . father . . .

**Regine** What's he been saying?

**Manders** He's confused me, totally.

**Engstrand** (*entering from hall*) Pastor Manders!

**Manders** Are you still following me?

**Engstrand** I've had to, Pastor! This whole . . . horrible . . . thing!

**Manders** I know.

**Engstrand** And a stupid little accident the cause of it, that's what gets me –

**Regine** What do you mean?

**Engstrand** Well it was the blessing that did it, sort of thing –

**Manders** Oh, good Lord.

**Engstrand** (*to Manders*) And to think I'm the one who brought you down there, and into all this trouble –

**Manders** Engstrand –

**Engstrand** Because no one but the Pastor touched the candles down there, and that's the truth of it, oh shame.

**Manders** I am telling you now, Engstrand, I don't remember holding a single candle.

**Engstrand** I do. Yep. With me own eyes I saw it, the Pastor took the candle, snuffed it, and threw the wick away in the wood shavings.

**Manders** You saw this?

**Engstrand** Saw it all.

**Manders** I'm not in the habit of . . . of snuffing out candles with my bare hands –

**Engstrand** It did look a bit . . . I was taken aback, if I'm honest but . . . You wouldn't have thought it could be so dangerous!

**Manders** Oh good God, this isn't real.

**Engstrand** And no insurance you're telling me?

**Manders** I told you, no.

**Engstrand** No insurance. And then you go and burn the place down, it's tragic that.

**Manders** Yes, it is.

*A short pause.*

**Engstrand** And not just any old spot, I mean a children's home! When you think of the kind of place it was meant to be, and the good it'd do for country and town, I mean – You don't come out of it well, Pastor. This whole shenanigan . . .

**Manders** No, I don't, Engstrand, thank you for clarifying.
    It's almost the worst thing about it, is how . . . is how people will use this against me now.

**Helen** (*entering from the garden*) He won't come away from the fire.

**Manders** There you are.

**Helen** So you didn't have to make a speech after all.

**Manders** I would have gladly made a speech, I . . .

**Helen** (*quietly*) All for the best. That place wouldn't have done any good for anyone. I'm sure of it.

**Manders** You believe that?

**Helen** Don't you?

**Manders** It's a tragedy, whichever way you look at it.

**Helen** It's a business matter now. That's all.
  Are you waiting for the Pastor, Engstrand?

**Engstrand** I am.

**Helen** Sit down for a while.

**Engstrand** I'd prefer to be upstanding, thank you.

**Helen** (*to Manders*) You're going to take the boat
tonight, I presume.

**Manders** There's one in an hour.

**Helen** Take all the papers with you, would you please?
I don't want to hear another word of all this. I've other
things to think of now.

**Manders** Helen . . .

**Helen** I'll send a letter on to you, a . . . to make you a
what's-it-called. To authorise you, to settle everything as
you like.

**Manders** I'd be happy, to be your executor, Helen.
  The legacy . . . will have to be changed completely now.

**Helen** Yes.

**Manders** The easiest thing, I suppose, is . . . I can
organise for the farm to go to the council. The land is
still worth something. Someone'll put it to some kind
of use, I could use the interest to . . . to support another
enterprise, of benefit to the town –

**Helen** Do what you like, Pastor Manders. I don't care.

**Engstrand** There is . . . the cultural centre, Pastor.

**Manders** Yes. Yes, that should definitely be on the table –

**Engstrand** (*in frustration*) 'On the table', he says –

**Manders** It mightn't be my decision, Engstrand.
Depending on what happens, with the inquest into the
all this, I might . . . be forced to consider my position.

**Helen** Why?

**Manders** No one knows how these things'll turn out.

**Engstrand** But in this case – with witness Engstrand on
call . . .

**Manders** What do you mean?

**Engstrand** And Jacob Engstrand is loyal to his friends,
and benefactors . . .
    He's got your back.

**Manders** I don't know how . . .
    Jacob I don't know what you / mean

**Engstrand** I'm an angel of salvation, me –

**Manders** No. No, I can't have –

**Engstrand** That's the way it is.
    I know someone who's taken my sins on his shoulders
a thousand times.
    And now I can repay him.

**Manders** Jacob . . .
    This is a fine man. A rare man.
    You'll have all the help you need, with this cultural
centre of yours, believe you me.

*Engstrand wants to thank him, but is overcome with
gratitude.*

**Engstrand** I . . .

**Manders** We'll take the boat together.
    God bless you, Jacob.

**Osvald** (*having entered from the garden*) God speed.

**Engstrand** (*at the dining-room door, quietly to Regine*) Live like a queen, you come back with me.

**Regine** Non merci!

**Engstrand** You know where to find me. Ever change your mind. Little Harbour Street.
(*To Helen and Osvald.*) And the centre, for the people of the town, and of the port will be called 'Captain Alving's House', by God it will. And if I can run the place as I feel to, I dare say . . . it'll be worthy of the man, and of his name.

**Manders** After you, Jacob.
Helen.

**Helen** Goodbye, Pastor Manders.

**Manders** Goodbye, all.

*Manders and Engstrand exit via the hall.*

**Osvald** What centre was he on about?

**Helen** It's more of a bar, I should think, for sailors.
Pastor Manders doesn't quite know what he's sponsoring.

**Osvald** It'll burn down anyway.

**Helen** What makes you say that?

**Osvald** Everything will. Everything to do with Father, anyway.
Even I'm burning.

*Regine looks at him, concerned.*

**Helen** Osvald! You shouldn't have stayed out in the cold so long.

**Osvald** You might be right.

**Helen** Wipe your face – Let me do it, Osvald, you're sweating.

**Osvald** (*indifferently*) Thank you, Mummy.

**Helen** Do you want to sleep?

**Osvald** (*afraid*) No! No, not sleep, I never sleep. I just pretend.
  There'll be enough time for sleeping soon.

**Helen** You look exhausted –

**Regine** Is Mr Alving sick?

**Osvald** Close the doors! Quickly!

*At a nod from Helen, Regine does so.*

I can feel it, I can feel this . . . fear again . . .

*Regine closes the door and remains in the doorway.
Helen takes off her scarf, as does Regine. Helen pulls
up a chair and sits by Osvald.*

**Helen** There. I'm right by your side.

**Osvald** Stay with me. Regine, you too. Regine must be
with me, always. You'll always be here to help me, won't
you, Regine?

**Regine** Mr Alving . . .

**Osvald** When it gets to that point. Do you know what
I mean by that?

**Helen** Osvald, your mother is here.

**Osvald** But you won't help me, will you, not when it
comes to it, you won't be able to . . . (*Half laughs.*) The
nearest and dearest. They're not much use in the end,
they never can.

**Helen** But what do you mean?

**Osvald** (*violently*) Why won't you speak to me, Regine? And call me Osvald.

**Regine** I don't think . . . that Mrs Alving –

**Helen** Come and sit with us, Regine.

*Regine sits down quietly and reluctantly at the other side of the table.*

I'm going to make you feel much better, Osvald.

**Osvald** Are you, Mother? How?

**Helen** I'm going to take away all of this anger and sadness and . . . recriminations –

**Osvald** Can you?

**Helen** I can. You talked about . . . the joy of being alive. And suddenly I saw my whole life, quite clearly.

**Osvald** Oh, I don't know what you're talking about –

**Helen** You should have seen your father when he was your age. Full of joy.

**Osvald** I know he was.

**Helen** As you said yourself, his warmth. It was sunlight, just to look at him. He was a force, he was . . . vitality.

**Osvald** When he was my age.

**Helen** Yes.

**Osvald** And then?

**Helen** And then this joyous child . . . and he was like a child, in those days . . . He was put to live here, in a small town without a purpose, all he had was a position to keep, and apart from that . . .

No work he could lose himself in.

And not a single friend, to share his passions with, he was reduced to . . . to spending his life with dropouts and addicts of all descriptions –

**Osvald** Mother are / you –

**Helen** You said yourself, you know what would happen if you had to stay here.

And that is what happened to him.

**Osvald** You're telling me . . . my father . . .

**Helen** He was a father not only to you, dear Osvald.

He strayed, away from me, I didn't bring any sunlight into his life, I'm afraid I couldn't.

They taught me about responsibility.

Everything eventually came down to duties. My duties. His.

I made the home unbearable, I think..

**Osvald** Why . . . You never told me this before –

**Helen** Because he was your father, and you his son, and I . . .

I painted my little picture of him, for you, didn't I?

I didn't want you to see . . .

**Osvald** To see the truth of my own . . .

**Helen** I didn't want you knowing.

And I knew that Regine . . .

That she deserved a place in this house, that she belonged here.

As much as you did.

As a daughter of this house, in fact.

**Osvald** Regine –?

**Regine** I . . .

*A pause.*

**Helen** And now you both know.

**Osvald** Regine?

**Regine** My mother . . .

**Helen** Your mother was a good woman, Regine.

**Regine** I often wondered.
About the kind of woman she was.

**Helen** She was a very good woman, in a good many ways.

**Regine** She was that kind of woman, it turns out.

**Helen** Regine –

**Regine** Would you mind . . . Mrs Alving, if I left for a while, now I mean?
I know it's late. But I'd appreciate . . .

**Helen** If that's really what you want –

**Regine** Yes, it really is.

*Osvald approaches Regine.*

**Osvald** This is your home.

**Regine** Merci, Mr Alving.
I can call you Osvald now.
Though not in the way I'd imagined it, but . . .

**Helen** I am sorry, Regine. I've misled you –

**Regine** No. No, you've been very kind.
If I'd known Osvald was ill, then . . .
But then nothing can happen between us anyway!
I can't stay here.
I'm sorry.
But . . . spending my days a nurse –

**Osvald**  Not even for your brother?

**Regine**  Not even for him.
  I haven't . . . much, but I'm still young.
  So I should go.
  The joy of life, Mrs Alving, I've heard about that.

**Helen**  Don't throw yourself away, Regine –

**Regine**  What else is there to do?
  I won't.
  Then again, if it's his father Osvald takes after . . .
perhaps I'm my mother's child –

**Helen**  Regine –

**Regine**  Does Pastor Manders know about me?

**Helen**  He knows it all.

**Regine**  Right.
  Well, in that case I think I'd better get the next boat.
  I think the Pastor will be kind to me.
  I think I've a right to that money. As much as that
degenerate has.

**Helen**  You're welcome to every penny of it, Regine.

  *Regine stares at Helen.*

**Regine**  You could have found a nice home, for a child, a
respectable father, that would have been . . .
  No.
  (*Staring at the unopened bottle.*) I'll drink champagne,
out of my own glass one day.

**Helen**  Come back to me, whenever you need.

**Regine**  Thank you, Mrs Alving.
  But I know a place for me, if I need it.
  Captain Alving's House, in Little Harbour Street.

**Helen**  Oh, promise me you won't end up there.

**Regine**  (*with frustration*) Oh . . . Adieu!

*She exits via the hall.*

**Osvald**  (*standing by the window*) Gone?

**Helen**  Yes.

**Osvald**  Wrong. It's all wrong.

*Helen goes behind him and puts her hands on his shoulders.*

**Helen**  Darling. It's such a thing to take in, I know it is.
I worried it would be too much for you.

**Osvald**  Too much . . . ?
You could say that.
But at the same time it's nothing.

**Helen**  Nothing?
To know . . . that your father was so unhappy?

**Osvald**  Oh . . . my father. I never knew the man!
I've lied to myself, I know nothing of him apart from what? He put a pipe in my mouth when I was five and made me puke.

**Helen**  You know what you felt for him all these years.
A child doesn't have to . . . to know its father to love him!

**Osvald**  When his father's given him nothing?
That is a superstition, Mother, and a dead one.

**Helen**  A superstition –?

**Osvald**  Oh, floating about from another age like . . .

**Helen**  A ghost.

**Osvald**  You could call it that.

**Helen** But then that means you don't love me, either.

**Osvald** I know you, at least.

**Helen** Is that all?

**Osvald** And I know . . . how much you care for me.
I suppose . . . I'm grateful for that.
 And now I'm ill . . .
 You can help me.

**Helen** Oh, I will, Osvald. I could almost bless your illness for bringing you home to me at last.

**Osvald** What?

**Helen** Because I see it now. You're not mine. I have to earn you.

**Osvald** Oh . . . enough. Mother, I'm sick, I can't think of other people, it's work enough to think of myself –

**Helen** I'll be anything you want me to be.

**Osvald** Then be happy, please.

**Helen** Yes!
 Yes, I'll be happy.
 (*Goes to him.*) Have I made things easier for you, Ossie?
 Have I taken away . . . some of those feelings of remorse, and . . . blame –

**Osvald** Thank you, Mother.
 But who will take away the fear?

**Helen** The fear?

**Osvald** (*moving away*) Regine would have done it.

**Helen** Regine?

 *A pause.*

**Osvald** Is it very late?

**Helen** It's early, now. I can see daybreak behind the mountains.

I can see a clear morning.

You'll see the sun today, Osvald.

**Osvald** Thank God for that.

There are so many things, to be alive for –

**Helen** (*in agreement*) Aren't there?

**Osvald** Even if I can't work, then –

**Helen** You'll work again soon, I know you will.

Now your mind is clear. And you know the truth.

**Osvald** The truth is good to know.

And now . . .

*He sits on the sofa.*

Can I talk to you, and . . . and let the sun rise – Yes? – all the while –

**Helen** Yes, let's.

**Osvald** And then you'll know.

And I won't have this fear any more.

**Helen** What will I know?

**Osvald** You said to me this evening. You said there was nothing you wouldn't do for me if I asked.

**Helen** I did.

**Osvald** And that was the truth?

**Helen** Only the truth.

I live for no one but you.

**Osvald** Yes. Good. That's good.

You're strong, Mother, I know you are, so you must be very brave –

**Helen** Osvald?

**Osvald** And you mustn't shout. Do you promise me?
We'll sit quietly, and talk. And we'll stay very calm –

**Helen** What is it?

**Osvald** This . . . tiredness I've talked about, it isn't the
only thing, with this condition. Not by a long way.
This disease, which is my inheritance, sits . . . here.
(*Points at his forehead.*) Waiting.

**Helen** Osvald –

**Osvald** (*silencing her*) No.
It can break out at any time.
And when it does . . . it's the end of everything.

**Helen** My child –

**Osvald** But this is the way it is, and I'm telling you . . .
I had one attack when I was abroad, it soon passed.
But the fear it gave birth to inside me, it . . .
That's what sent me back to you.

**Helen** The fear of it returning.

**Osvald** If it was any other condition or illness or . . .
It's not even a fear of death, I'm not afraid to die . . .
Not that I wouldn't mind living –

**Helen** Of course!

**Osvald** But to turn back into a baby . . .
To have . . . spoons shoved in my mouth, my arse
wiped –

**Helen** Your mother is here.

**Osvald** And that's exactly what I don't want.
For years and years.
You might even go before I do.

It might not be fatal at first, look it up.
It's in the brain, the doctor said, it's . . . a softening.
(*Smiles, sadly.*) I thought it sounds quite beautiful.
Cherry-red velvet, it made me think of . . .
Draped all over me.

**Helen**  Osvald.

**Osvald**  You sent Regine away.
She would have done it for me.

**Helen**  What on earth could she have done that I can't?

**Osvald**  The next attack, the doctor said, will be the
turning point.

**Helen**  How could they have told you that –

**Osvald**  Because it's the truth?
Because I made them tell me.
Told him I had arrangements to make.

*He pulls a little box out of his inner breast pocket.*

You see this?

**Helen**  What is it?

**Osvald**  Twelve little pills all ready.

**Helen**  Give those to me!

**Osvald**  Not yet, Mother.

*He puts it away.*

**Helen**  You're going to be the death of me.

**Osvald**  I hope not. You have to help me.
Regine would have done it, I know she would.

**Helen**  Regine is a kind girl –

**Osvald**  Then she'd have done it out of kindness. And if
she's not, then . . . then out of disgust.

**Helen**  Never.

**Osvald**  At a disgusting . . . incapable –

**Helen**  Then thank God she isn't here.

**Osvald**  And it's down to you.

**Helen**  I'm your mother!

**Osvald**  Exactly.

**Helen**  I'm the one who gave you life!

**Osvald**  I didn't ask you for it!
I don't want this life, take it back!

**Helen**  Somebody help me . . .

*She runs out to the hall.*

**Osvald**  Where are you going?

**Helen**  To get the doctor for you, Osvald –

**Osvald**  No one is coming. And we're staying here.

*He locks the door.*

**Helen**  (*entering again*) Osvald.

**Osvald**  A mother's love. Not all it's cracked up to be is
it, then, if it sits back and watches me suffer.

*A pause.*

**Helen**  Here is my hand.

**Osvald**  You . . . ?

**Helen**  If it becomes necessary.
But it won't do, it can't . . .
It isn't possible –

**Osvald**  Oh no, it won't, and isn't, and . . .
Let's live together as long as we can.

*He sits down in the armchair which Helen had moved to the sofa.*

**Helen** (*moves closer, cautiously*) Do you feel more calm?

**Osvald** Yes, Mother.

**Helen** You've imagined these things, Osvald. Just imagined them.
But you can rest now.
At home with your mother.
You'll have everything you want, like when you were a child.
That . . . was an attack just then, wasn't it?
And it came and went.
Do you see how easy it was?
And do you see, Osvald . . . what a lovely day we'll have.
The sun will shine so bright.
Now you can really see your home.

*She goes to the table and puts out the lamp.*
*Sunrise.*
*The glacier and the peaks in the background gleam in the sunlight.*
*Osvald sits in the armchair with his back to the background, without moving. Suddenly, he says –*

**Osvald** Mother, give me the sun.

**Helen** (*looks at him, a little puzzled*) What's that?

**Osvald** The sun. The sun.

**Helen** Osvald what are you feeling?

*Osvald goes limp, all his muscles relaxed. He stares straight ahead.*

Osvald? Osvald! Osvald, don't you recognise me?!

**Osvald** (*as before*) The sun.

**Helen** I can't bear it, I can't! Where did he . . .

*She searches his pockets. Finds the box.*

Here!

*She retreats a few paces.*

No. No. No . . .
Yes.
No, no!

*She stands a few steps away from him. She stares at him, in speechless terror.*

**Osvald** (*as before*) The sun.
The sun.

*The End.*